Comprehensive PHP PEAR::DB

Blake Schwendiman

COPYRIGHT V

TRADEMARKS... V

DEVELOPER-FRIENDLY REQUEST VI

DOCUMENT CONVENTIONS..................................... VI

ABOUT THE AUTHOR.. VI

PEAR AND DATABASES.. 1

MOTIVATION FOR THIS DOCUMENT 1
GETTING STARTED 1
WHAT THIS BOOK IS NOT... 2
  Installing PEAR 2
  Installing PEAR::DB 8

OVERVIEW OF PEAR::DB....................................... 8

PROCEDURAL DB ACCESS VS. PEAR::DB 8
  Procedural DB Access 11
  PEAR::DB.. 13
SOFTWARE ENGINEERING AND PEAR::DB 14
SUMMARY 16

PEAR::DB IN DEPTH... 17

INTRODUCTION 17
  DSN 17
  Connect 19
  Query... 22
  Fetch 22
  Sequences.. 22
  Prepare and Execute.. 26
  autoPrepare and autoExecute.. 27
  Introductory Summary... 29
CLASS DB... 29
  DB::factory.. 30
  DB::connect... 32
  DB::apiVersion.. 34
  DB::isError 34
  DB::isConnection... 34
  DB::isWarning.. 34
  DB::isManip... 35
  DB::errorMessage 35
  DB::parseDSN.. 35
  DB::assertExtension... 36

Class DB Summary *37*
CLASS DB_COMMON *37*
DB_common::toString *42*
DB_common::quoteString *42*
DB_common::quote *43*
DB_common::provides *44*
DB_common::errorCode *46*
DB_common::errorMessage *47*
DB_common::raiseError *47*
DB_common::setFetchMode *52*
DB_common::setOption *59*
DB_common::getOption *59*
DB_common::prepare *60*
DB_common::autoPrepare *63*
DB_common::autoExecute *66*
DB_common::buildManipSQL *67*
DB_common::execute *68*
DB_common::executeEmulateQuery *69*
DB_common::executeMultiple *70*
DB_common::freePrepared *71*
DB_common::modifyQuery *72*
DB_common::modifyLimitQuery *72*
DB_common::query *72*
DB_common::limitQuery *74*
DB_common::getOne *76*
DB_common::getRow *78*
DB_common::getCol *79*
DB_common::getAssoc *81*
DB_common::getAll *90*
DB_common::autoCommit *93*
DB_common::commit *93*
DB_common::rollback *96*
DB_common::numRows *98*
DB_common::affectedRows *99*
DB_common::errorNative *100*
DB_common::nextId *100*
DB_common::createSequence *101*
DB_common::dropSequence *102*
DB_common::tableInfo *102*
DB_common::getTables *105*
DB_common::getListOf *106*
DB_common::getSequenceName *108*
CLASS DB_RESULT *109*
DB_result::setOption *110*

DB_result::fetchRow *110*
DB_result::fetchInto *113*
DB_result::numCols *114*
DB_result::numRows *115*
DB_result::nextResult *115*
DB_result::free *115*
DB_result::tableInfo *116*
DB_result::getRowCounter *121*
CLASS DB_ERROR 121
CLASS DB_WARNING 121
CLASS DB_STORAGE 122
DB_storage::_makeWhere *125*
DB_storage::setup *125*
DB_storage::insert *127*
DB_storage::toString *128*
DB_storage::dump *129*
DB_storage::create *130*
DB_storage::set *130*
DB_storage::get *131*
DB_storage::store *133*
DB_storage::remove *133*

DATABASE SUPPORT **134**

MYSQL 145
POSTGRESQL 146
BORLAND INTERBASE 146
MINI SQL 147
MICROSOFT SQL SERVER 148
ORACLE 7/8/8I 148
ODBC 149
SYBASE 150
INFORMIX 150
FRONTBASE 150
SQLITE 151
DBASE 152
DATABASE SUPPORT SUMMARY 153

CONCLUSION **154**

APPENDIX A: LISTS OF FIGURES **155**

TABLES 155
FIGURES 155
CODE LISTINGS 155
OUTPUT LISTINGS 158

INDEX 160

Copyright

Trademarks

The author has made every reasonable attempt to credit the appropriate trademark and/or registered trademark holders throughout this document.

Windows® is a registered trademark of Microsoft Corporation in the United States and other countries.

Borland®, the Borland Logo and Interbase® are trademarks or registered trademarks of Borland Software Corporation in the United States and other countries.

MySQL® is a registered trademark of MySQL AB in the United States, the European Union and other countries.

Oracle® is a registered trademark of Oracle Corporation.

Sybase and the SYBASE logo are trademarks of Sybase, Inc. or its subsidiaries.

Informix® is a registered trademark of International Business Machines Corporation in the United States, other countries, or both.

FrontBase™ is a trademark of FrontBase, Inc.

Developer-friendly Request

If you have received a copy of this document electronically and you have not paid for it, please consider purchasing a licensed copy. A great deal of time and effort went into the creation of this document and if it has provided you with any useful information, visit **http://www.intechra.net/** for details on purchasing this document. The more developers who support this type of documentation, the better the documentation will become.

Document Conventions

➲ Within a function or method description, the return value is identified using the arrow notation associated with this paragraph.

〰 Paragraphs with the squiggly to the left typically represent my personal recommendations or personal thoughts on a topic.

About the Author

This is my third PHP-related title, the second that is self-published. As a developer, it's always been challenging to me to find the right level of documentation for the right price. This title and my other, *Building Custom PHP Extensions*, are books that I've wanted to write for some time, covering interesting PHP topics and doing so at an affordable price.

I'm considering titles all the time. If you like this book (or if you hate it), drop me a line. You'll find my contact information at http://www.intechra.net/. Let me know if you have a specific topic you'd like to see covered.

PEAR and Databases

Motivation for this Document

PEAR is about code reuse. That's the primary motivation for this document. If you're a PHP programmer and you've developed any database projects, PEAR::DB is for you. Over the lifetime of PHP there have been several great database abstractions developed, some OO, some not. PEAR::DB is **the** standard object oriented database abstraction.

As PHP continues to evolve and grow in its user base, more and more developers will be hired to maintain and modify existing code. By standardizing on PEAR, maintenance and upgrades will focus on business-specific code and not general-purpose code such as database access.

Getting Started

This book assumes a great deal about you as a programmer. First, you must have PHP installed and running on your web server. Second, this book assumes that you have a general working knowledge of PHP. There are many fantastic *getting started* documents available out there if you need more information about installing and using PHP in general. Third, it is assumed that you have a database server installed, configured and running.

What This Book is Not

This book is not a best practices book or a software engineering primer. Most of the examples provided herein are incomplete in terms of proper HTML, error handling and output. The examples are typically intended to illustrate usage and are therefore short – focusing on tasks, not complete solutions.

Installing PEAR

Depending on your PHP version and your computing platform, there may be some steps needed to install and configure PEAR.

If you are running a version of PHP prior to version 4.3, you will likely need to manually install the PEAR package manager. Later versions of PHP (4.3 and higher) come with the PEAR package manager or the package manager is built be default. If you added the **--without-pear** flag to your configuration of PHP, you will also need to get the PEAR package manager.

For Unix, Linux and BSD you can obtain the PEAR package manager using the command line:

```
1    lynx -source http://go-pear.org/ | php
```

The above command line requires that you have lynx installed (it may be called *links* on some Linux distributions). It is also assumed that you have your PHP binary built and installed.

For Windows users, there is a similar tool in the standard source distribution called **go-pear.bat**.

Running this batch file will walk you through the PEAR installation process. This batch file is very complete and will perform almost all of the necessary tasks of updating your Windows system to use PEAR. The only step required after running the batch file is to add to the PATH environment variable.

The first step is to locate the **pear.bat** file. It will be located in the directory you specified when running the **go-pear.bat** batch file. After locating the **pear.bat** file, add its directory to the PATH environment variable in Windows. This is done by right-clicking the *My Computer* icon. Select *Properties* from the context menu, and then click the *Advanced* tab. A screen shot (Windows XP) is shown below in Figure 1.

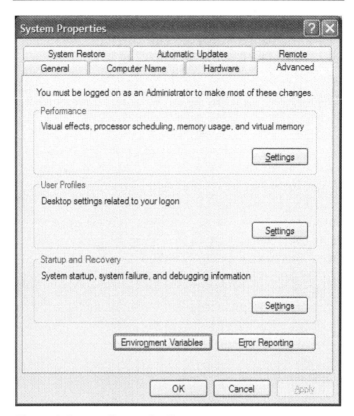

Figure 1: System Properties Page

Next, click the *Environment Variables* button to add the new environment variable. Figure 2 shows the dialog that allows the creation and modification of system environment variables.

Scroll through the *System variables* until you locate the *Path* variable. Then click the *Edit* button to add the new directory to the end. In Windows, path items are separated by semicolons.

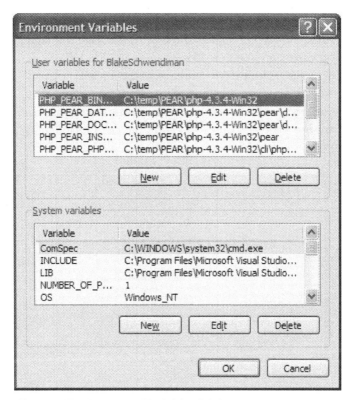

Figure 2: Environment Variables Dialog

Figure 3 shows how the Path variable looks on my computer after adding the directory containing the **pear.bat** file.

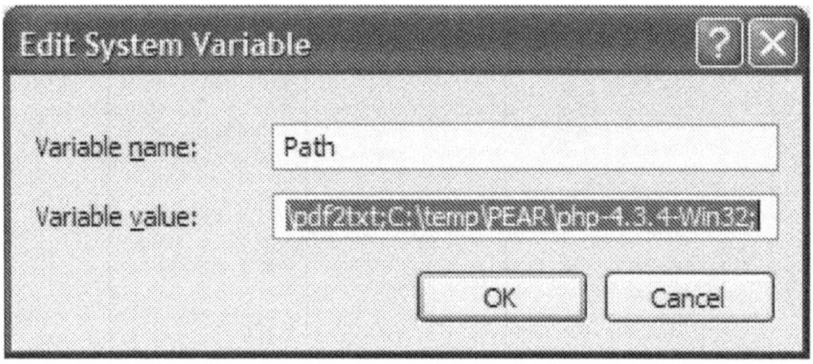

Figure 3: Adding the Path to the PEAR.BAT File

Once you have installed the PEAR package manager, you can begin using it to manage your PEAR packages. The PEAR package manager is invoked using the command **pear**. Assuming you have properly installed and configured your environment, running this command will produce the output shown in Output 1 below.

```
1  Usage: pearcmd.php [options] command [command-
   options] <parameters>
2  Type "pearcmd.php help options" to list all
   options.
3  Type "pearcmd.php help <command>" to get the help
   for the specified command.
4  Commands:
5  build                   Build an Extension From C
   Source
6  bundle                  Unpacks a Pecl Package
7  clear-cache             Clear XML-RPC Cache
8  config-get              Show One Setting
9  config-help             Show Information About
   Setting
10 config-set              Change Setting
11 config-show             Show All Settings
12 cvsdiff                 Run a "cvs diff" for all
   files in a package
13 cvstag                  Set CVS Release Tag
14 download                Download Package
15 download-all            Downloads each avaible
   Package from master_server
16 info                    Display information about a
   package
17 install                 Install Package
18 list                    List Installed Packages
19 list-all                List All Packages
20 list-upgrades           List Available Upgrades
21 login                   Connects and authenticates
   to remote server
22 logout                  Logs out from the remote
   server
23 makerpm                 Builds an RPM spec file from
   a PEAR package
24 package                 Build Package
25 package-dependencies    Show package dependencies
26 package-validate        Validate Package Consistency
27 remote-info             Information About Remote
   Packages
28 remote-list             List Remote Packages
29 run-tests               Run Regression Tests
30 search                  Search remote package
   database
31 shell-test              Shell Script Test
32 sign                    Sign a package distribution
   file
33 uninstall               Un-install Package
```

```
34   upgrade                Upgrade Package
35   upgrade-all            Upgrade All Packages
```

Output 1: Running the PEAR command with no command-line arguments

The PEAR package manager is a powerful tool for installing, removing, updating and testing your PEAR configuration. To see which PEAR packages are currently installed, use the following syntax:

```
1   pear list
```

On a new installation of PEAR, the output will look something like that shown below in Output 2.

```
2    INSTALLED PACKAGES:
3    ====================
4    PACKAGE          VERSION         STATE
5    Archive_Tar      1.1             stable
6    Console_Getopt   1.0             stable
7    DB               1.5.0RC2        stable
8    Mail             1.1.2           stable
9    Net_SMTP         1.2.3           stable
10   Net_Socket       1.0.1           stable
11   PEAR             1.3b1           beta
12   PHPUnit          1.0.0-alpha2    alpha
13   XML_Parser       1.0.1           stable
14   XML_RPC          1.0.4           stable
```

Output 2: Output of PEAR LIST

As can be seen, the Archive_Tar, Console_Getopt, DB, Mail, Net_SMTP, Net_Socket, PEAR, PHPUnit, XML_Parser and XLM_RPC classes are installed. The version numbers and state of each package are also available.

Installing PEAR::DB

If you do not have the DB package installed, using the following command to install DB:

```
1    pear install DB
```

If you do not have the most current version of DB or if you need to check for an upgrade and install it, use:

```
1    pear upgrade DB
```

Note that the above will cause an upgrade to be installed if one exists. If you simply wish to check for upgrades, use the **pear list-all** or **pear list-upgrades** commands.

For the purposes of this document, it will be assumed that the version of PEAR::DB is 1.5.0RC2.

Overview of PEAR::DB

To begin, this section illustrates the core concepts of PEAR::DB by providing a comparison of procedural database access in PHP and OO database access using PEAR::DB.

Procedural DB Access vs. PEAR::DB

This section shows the similarities and the differences between using procedural database access and PEAR::DB. The example is deliberately simple, showing how to establish a database connection, retrieve a small recordset and close the connection.

The example uses MySQL as the database backend, but could conceivably be any PHP-supported database.

For the examples, a simple four-table database will be used to illustrate a small employee and department data set. The four tables are *Employees*, *Paychecks*, *EmployeesToDepartments*, and *Departments*. The MySQL queries to create and populate the tables are shown below in Code Listing 1.

```
1   #
2   # Table structure for table `Departments`
3   #
4
5   CREATE TABLE `Departments` (
6     `id` int(11) NOT NULL default '0',
7     `name` varchar(50) NOT NULL default '',
8     PRIMARY KEY  (`id`)
9   ) TYPE=MyISAM;
10
11  #
12  # Dumping data for table `Departments`
13  #
14
15  INSERT INTO `Departments` VALUES (1, 'Web
    Development');
16  INSERT INTO `Departments` VALUES (2, 'QA');
17
18  # -----------------------------------------------
    -------
19
20  #
21  # Table structure for table `Employees`
22  #
23
24  CREATE TABLE `Employees` (
25    `id` int(11) NOT NULL default '0',
26    `last_name` varchar(50) NOT NULL default '',
27    `first_name` varchar(50) NOT NULL default '',
28    `phone_ext` varchar(5) NOT NULL default '',
29    `mgr_id` int(11) NOT NULL default '0',
30    `dept_id` int(11) NOT NULL default '0',
31    PRIMARY KEY  (`id`),
32    KEY `mgr_id` (`mgr_id`),
33    KEY `dept_id` (`dept_id`)
34  ) TYPE=InnoDB;
35
36  #
37  # Dumping data for table `Employees`
38  #
39
40  INSERT INTO `Employees` VALUES (1, 'Schwendiman',
    'Blake', '204', 2, 1);
```

```
41  INSERT INTO `Employees` VALUES (2, 'Cox',
    'Jeffrey', '225', 0, 1);
42  INSERT INTO `Employees` VALUES (3, 'McNulty',
    'Kate', '214', 2, 2);
43
44  #
45  # Table structure for table `Paychecks`
46  #
47
48  CREATE TABLE `Paychecks` (
49    `id` int(11) NOT NULL auto_increment,
50    `employee_id` int(11) NOT NULL default '0',
51    `check_date` date NOT NULL default '0000-00-00',
52    `check_number` int(11) NOT NULL default '0',
53    `gross_pay` float NOT NULL default '0',
54    `benefits_withheld` float NOT NULL default '0',
55    `taxes_withheld` float NOT NULL default '0',
56    PRIMARY KEY (`id`)
57  ) TYPE=MyISAM AUTO_INCREMENT=1 ;
58
59  CREATE TABLE `EmployeesToDepartments` (
60    `emp_id` int(11) NOT NULL default '0',
61    `dept_id` int(11) NOT NULL default '0',
62    `date_xferred` date NOT NULL default '0000-00-
    00',
63    PRIMARY KEY (`emp_id`,`dept_id`)
64  ) TYPE=MyISAM;
```

Code Listing 1: MySQL Statements to Create Sample Database

The *Employees* table contains a field called *dept_id* representing the current department in which the employee works. The *EmployeesToDepartments* table is an intermediate table to effect an m-to-n relationship between *Employees* and *Departments* representing historical information about which employees have ever worked in a department. The real purpose of the *EmployeesToDepartments* table, though, is for examples in which a multiple-field key is needed.

The sample code will use the SQL query shown in Code Listing 2 below to retrieve data about employees, their department and their manager. The query is deliberately more complex than the most basic SELECT statement to provide more value to the example, but the details of the SQL statement will not be covered in this document.

```
1   SELECT Employees.last_name as emp_last_name,
    Employees.first_name as emp_first_name,
    Employees.phone_ext as emp_phone_ext,
    Departments.name as dept_name,
    Employees_1.last_name as mgr_last_name,
    Employees_1.first_name as mgr_first_name,
    Employees_1.phone_ext as mgr_phone_ext FROM
    (Departments INNER JOIN Employees ON Departments.id
    = Employees.dept_id) LEFT JOIN Employees AS
    Employees_1 ON Employees.mgr_id = Employees_1.id
```

Code Listing 2: SQL Query for Sample Employee Database

Both the procedural example and the PEAR::DB
example will retrieve the data and create an HTML
table containing the results.

Procedural DB Access

The code in the example below (Code Listing 3)
illustrates the common procedural method for
retrieving data from a MySQL database.

```php
1   <?php
2     // connect to MySQL DB
3     $link = mysql_pconnect( '207.44.182.3',
    'bt_user', 'bt_pass' );
4     if ( $link !== FALSE )
5     {
6       if ( mysql_select_db( 'book_test' ) )
7       {
8
9         /* Performing SQL query */
10        $query = "SELECT Employees.last_name as
    emp_last_name, Employees.first_name as
    emp_first_name, Employees.phone_ext as
    emp_phone_ext, Departments.name as dept_name,
    Employees_1.last_name as mgr_last_name,
    Employees_1.first_name as mgr_first_name,
    Employees_1.phone_ext as mgr_phone_ext FROM
    (Departments INNER JOIN Employees ON Departments.id
    = Employees.dept_id) LEFT JOIN Employees AS
    Employees_1 ON Employees.mgr_id = Employees_1.id";
11        $result = mysql_query($query);
12
13        if ( $result !== FALSE )
14        {
15          /* Printing results in HTML */
16          print '<table>';
```

```
17        while ( $line = mysql_fetch_array( $result,
MYSQL_ASSOC ) )
18          {
19            print '<tr>';
20            foreach ( $line as $col_value ) {
21              print "<td>$col_value</td>";
22            }
23            print '</tr>';
24          }
25          print '</table>';
26        }
27        else
28        {
29          print( 'Query failed: ' );
30          print( mysql_error() );
31          print( '<br>' );
32        }
33
34        /* Free resultset */
35        mysql_free_result($result);
36      }
37      else
38      {
39        print( 'Unable to select database
<i>book_test</i>: ' );
40        print( mysql_error() );
41        print( '<br>' );
42      }
43
44      /* Closing connection */
45      mysql_close($link);
46    }
47    else
48    {
49      print( 'Unable to connect to database server: '
);
50      print( mysql_error() );
51      print( '<br>' );
52    }
53  ?>
```

Code Listing 3: Procedural DB Access

Experienced PHP developers will see the common
elements in the code above. Line 3 is the call to
establish a connection to the database server. On
success, the code at line 6 selects the particular
database. The SELECT query is issued to the
database on line 11 and if it succeeds, line 17 begins a
loop to retrieve all of the data from the result set and
process it for HTML output. In the event of a failure
at any point, the relevant failure information is
displayed to the end user.

PEAR::DB

The example above, recoded for PEAR::DB is shown in Code Listing 4.

```php
1   <?php
2     require_once( 'DB.php' );
3
4     $oDB = DB::connect(
      'mysql://bt_user:bt_pass@207.44.182.3/book_test',
      true );
5     if ( !DB::isError( $oDB ) )
6     {
7       $oDB->setFetchMode( DB_FETCHMODE_ASSOC );
8
9       $query = "SELECT Employees.last_name as
      emp_last_name, Employees.first_name as
      emp_first_name, Employees.phone_ext as
      emp_phone_ext, Departments.name as dept_name,
      Employees_1.last_name as mgr_last_name,
      Employees_1.first_name as mgr_first_name,
      Employees_1.phone_ext as mgr_phone_ext FROM
      (Departments INNER JOIN Employees ON Departments.id
      = Employees.dept_id) LEFT JOIN Employees AS
      Employees_1 ON Employees.mgr_id = Employees_1.id";
10
11      $oRows = $oDB->query( $query );
12      if ( !DB::isError( $oRows ) )
13      {
14        print( '<table>' );
15        while ( $oRow = $oRows->fetchRow() )
16        {
17          print '<tr>';
18          foreach ( $oRow as $col_value ) {
19            print "<td>$col_value</td>";
20          }
21          print '</tr>';
22        }
23        print( '</table>' );
24      }
25      else
26      {
27        print( 'Query failed: ' );
28        print( $oDB->getMessage() );
29        print( '<br>' );
30      }
31    }
32    else
33    {
34      print( 'Unable to connect to database server: '
      );
35      print( $oDB->getMessage() );
36      print( '<br>' );
37    }
38  ?>
```

Code Listing 4: PEAR::DB Database Access

Without going into a deep description of the methods used at this point, the above example illustrates connecting to and selecting a database in line 4. The query is issued in line 11 and the data is retrieved in the loop starting on line 15. The points of note are the connection mechanism and error handling.

Using PEAR::DB, the connection is made using the DB::connect method for all database server types. The first parameter is a *Data Source Name* (DSN) that will be described later. Most of the methods return a DB_Error object on failure to provide standardized error handling. This will also be described in depth later in this document.

Software Engineering and PEAR::DB

Using PEAR::DB does not fundamentally change the way one thinks about developing database applications in PHP, but it accomplishes several objectives critical to maintainable software development:

1. PEAR::DB promotes code re-use. Software developers that standardize on PEAR::DB will find that the database access portions of their projects will become more maintainable and easier to develop initially.
2. PEAR::DB provides a consistent interface to several database servers. Currently PEAR::DB supports MySQL, PostgreSQL, InterBase, Mini SQL, Microsoft SQL Server, Oracle 7/8/8i, ODBC, SyBase, Informix, SQLite, FrontBase and dBase. More back

ends are likely to be supported in future PEAR::DB releases.

3. PEAR::DB provides a consistent interface to error handling through the DB_Error class (a subclass of the PEAR_Error class).

As a software developer, it is nearly impossible to overstate the benefits of standardizing and reusing software components over multiple development projects. If there were no other reason to use PEAR::DB, it would still be worthwhile to every PHP developer just from a reuse perspective alone. There are more reasons to use PEAR::DB, though, and all of these will be explored through the remainder of this document.

The following example should be enough reason for any PHP developer to get excited about PEAR::DB. The code in Code Listing 5 below is an exact duplicate of Code Listing 4, but with the DSN changed on line 4. This simple change in the code has dramatic effects on the run-time behavior of the script. Instead of using MySQL, this script uses ODBC to connect to a Microsoft Access database to retrieve the necessary data.

```
1   <?php
2     require_once( 'DB.php' );
3
4     $oDB = DB::connect( 'odbc://book_test', true );
5     if ( !DB::isError( $oDB ) )
6     {
7       $oDB->setFetchMode( DB_FETCHMODE_ASSOC );
8
9       $query = "SELECT Employees.last_name as
      emp_last_name, Employees.first_name as
      emp_first_name, Employees.phone_ext as
      emp_phone_ext, Departments.name as dept_name,
      Employees_1.last_name as mgr_last_name,
      Employees_1.first_name as mgr_first_name,
      Employees_1.phone_ext as mgr_phone_ext FROM
      (Departments INNER JOIN Employees ON Departments.id
      = Employees.dept_id) LEFT JOIN Employees AS
      Employees_1 ON Employees.mgr_id = Employees_1.id";
10
```

```
11      $oRows = $oDB->query( $query );
12      if ( !DB::isError( $oRows ) )
13      {
14        print( '<table>' );
15        while ( $oRow = $oRows->fetchRow() )
16        {
17          print '<tr>';
18          foreach ( $oRow as $col_value ) {
19            print "<td>$col_value</td>";
20          }
21          print '</tr>';
22        }
23        print( '</table>' );
24      }
25      else
26      {
27        print( 'Query failed: ' );
28        print( $oDB->getMessage() );
29        print( '<br>' );
30      }
31    }
32    else
33    {
34      print( 'Unable to connect to database server: ' );
35      print( $oDB->getMessage() );
36      print( '<br>' );
37    }
38  ?>
```

Code Listing 5: PEAR::DB Database Access (Take Two)

The only external requirements to using the examples in Code Listing 4 and Code Listing 5 are that the databases must exist. The Microsoft Access database must have an ODBC DSN (specifically, a system DSN named *book_test*) set up to point to it as well.

Summary

No matter the size, scope or requirements of your PHP database application, PEAR::DB is applicable. It provides a consistent, easy-to-read interface to the major database back ends. It standardizes error handling and overall it simplifies the maintenance of PHP applications.

PEAR::DB In Depth

This section is the detailed reference section intended to provide the in-depth coverage of PEAR::DB and its classes.

Introduction

Before detailing the classes themselves, it is important to gain a high-level perspective of some of the concepts of using PEAR::DB. These concepts include the Data Source Name (DSN) and generally the methods need to connect to databases and retrieve or modify data. Another high-level concept covered in this section is sequences.

DSN

To connect to a database using PEAR::DB, you must first create a valid Data Source Name (DSN). For Windows users, it is important to distinguish between a PEAR::DB DSN and an ODBC DSN. An ODBC DSN may be used with a PEAR::DB DSN, but for most database types, the PEAR::DB DSN has nothing at all to do with an ODBC DSN. For details about using an ODBC database with PEAR::DB, see the ODBC section in the detailed examples starting on page 134.

A PEAR::DB DSN is formatted after the fashion of a Universal Resource Identifier. The format, in its fullest form is shown below in Code Listing 6.

```
1    phptype(dbsyntax)://username:password@protocol+host
     spec/database
```

Code Listing 6: Full DSN Format

Most variations are allowed, such as those shown
below in Code Listing 7.

```
2   phptype://username:password@protocol+hostspec:110//
    usr/db_file.db
3   phptype://username:password@hostspec/database_name
4   phptype://username:password@hostspec
5   phptype://username@hostspec
6   phptype://hostspec/database
7   phptype://hostspec
8   phptype(dbsyntax)
9   phptype
```

Code Listing 7: Variations of DSN Format

Currently, the following databases shown in Table 1
below are supported by PEAR::DB.

Database	phptype	Database Information Web Site
MySQL	mysql	http://www.mysql.com/
PostgreSQL	pgsql	http://www.postgresql.org/
Borland InterBase	ibase	http://www.borland.com/
Mini SQL	msql	http://www.hughes.com.au/products/msql
Microsoft SQL Server	mssql	http://www.microsoft.com/
Oracle 7/8/8i	oci8	http://www.oracle.com/
ODBC (Open Database Connectivity)	odbc	
SyBase	sybase	http://www.sybase.com/home
Informix	ifx	http://www.informix.com/
FrontBase	fbsql	http://www.frontbase.com

| SQLite | sqlite | http://www.sqlite.org/ |
| dBase | dbase | |

Table 1: PEAR::DB Supported Databases

Some examples of DSNs have already been shown in Code Listing 4 and Code Listing 5. Since the use of a DSN is so fundamental to using PEAR::DB, more examples will be given. Additionally in the detailed database-specific examples provided later, specific examples of a DSN for each supported database type will be provided.

Connect

Establishing a connection to any supported database is most easily accomplished using **DB::connect()**. There are two parameters: the connect DSN and a mixed value containing either a Boolean value or an array of values – this will be discussed further in this section. The return value of a call to **DB::connect()** is either a valid instance of a database class or an error or warning object. To check for errors and warnings, use the **DB::isError()** and **DB::isWarning()** class methods. To disconnect from the database, use the **disconnect()** method of the database object that is returned.

The second parameter to **DB::connect()** is important to understand, because it controls database specific options. Each database class type contains a **setOption()** method that is used to set various database specific optional values. The parent class of all the database classes, DB_common, defines the options shown in by default.

Option Name	Default Value	Brief Description
persistent	false	Whether or not to establish a persistent connection to the database.
optimize	performance	Values currently used are 'performance' and 'portability'. Each database uses this option in a slightly different way.
debug	0	Numeric value representing the level of debug information to generate.
seqname_format	%s_seq	Describes the format of the names used for sequences.
autofree	false	If set to **true**, this flag causes PEAR::DB to free all fetched data retrieved using fetchRow() or fetchInto().

Table 2: Default Options for Database Classes

For each option specified in the call to **DB::connect()**, the **setOption()** method is called once. If you do not specify any options, the default values are used. More details about the options can be found in the detailed coverage of each database starting on page 134. The *seqname_format* option will be discussed in the section on sequences.

It is also possible to pass a Boolean value instead of an array of values as the second parameter to **DB::connect()**. When a Boolean value is passed, it represents the value of the *persistent* option which indicates whether or not a persistent connection to the database should be established.

The sample code shown below in Code Listing 8 illustrates several examples of connections to a MySQL database server. No significant output is generated; this example is for illustration only.

```
1   <?php
2     require_once( 'DB.php' );
3
4     // make a non-persistent connection to a MySQL
      database
5     $oDB = DB::connect(
      'mysql://bt_user:bt_pass@207.44.182.3/book_test',
      false );
6     if ( !DB::isError( $oDB ) )
7     {
8       print( 'test 1 success<br>' );
9       $oDB->disconnect();
10    }
11
12    // make a persistent connection to a MySQL
      database
13    $oDB = DB::connect(
      'mysql://bt_user:bt_pass@207.44.182.3/book_test',
      true );
14    if ( !DB::isError( $oDB ) )
15    {
16      print( 'test 2 success<br>' );
17      $oDB->disconnect();
18    }
19
20    // make a persistent connection to a MySQL
      database -- alternate method
21    $oDB = DB::connect(
      'mysql://bt_user:bt_pass@207.44.182.3/book_test',
      array( 'persistent' => true ) );
22    if ( !DB::isError( $oDB ) )
23    {
24      print( 'test 3 success<br>' );
25      $oDB->disconnect();
```

```
26    }
27
28    // make a persistent connection to a MySQL
      database, set optimize to 'portability', increase
      debug level
29    $oDB = DB::connect(
      'mysql://bt_user:bt_pass@207.44.182.3/book_test',
      array( 'persistent' => true, 'optimize' =>
      'portability', 'debug' => 5 ) );
30    if ( !DB::isError( $oDB ) )
31    {
32       print( 'test 4 success<br>' );
33       $oDB->disconnect();
34    }
35    ?>
```

Code Listing 8: Examples of DB::connect()

Query

To perform a query against a database, use the
query() method. A simple example of using the
query() method is shown in Code Listing 4.
Complete details about this method are given in the
discussion of the **DB_common** class below.

Fetch

After performing a query that returns a data set, there
are two basic methods of retrieving the data,
fetchRow() and **fetchInto()**. Both of these methods
are described in detail in the discussion of the
DB_result class starting on page 109. For a simple
example of using **fetchRow()**, see Code Listing 4.

Sequences

Sequences are a way of maintaining unique numeric
IDs for data rows in a table. Several database servers

provide the concept of an automatically incrementing counter as a table column type. Sequences are a generalization of this concept.

Some database engines provide native support for sequences (such as Oracle). Other database types simply provide the automatically incrementing column type as mentioned above. In some cases, using such a column type introduces challenges into data recovery and importing. By using PEAR::DB sequences, code is more portable and maintainable and PEAR::DB sequences can avoid some of the problems associated with automatically incrementing fields.

A simple example of using a sequence is shown in Code Listing 9 below.

```php
1    <?php
2       require_once( 'DB.php' );
3
4       // make a non-persistent connection to a MySQL
     database
5       $oDB = DB::connect(
     'mysql://bt_user:bt_pass@207.44.182.3/book_test',
     false );
6       if ( !DB::isError( $oDB ) )
7       {
8          $idSeq1 = $oDB->nextId( 'sequence_1' );
9          print( "idSeq1 = $idSeq1<br>" );
10
11         $idSeq1 = $oDB->nextId( 'sequence_1' );
12         print( "idSeq1 = $idSeq1<br>" );
13
14         $idSeq2 = $oDB->nextId( 'sequence_2' );
15         print( "idSeq2 = $idSeq2<br>" );
16
17         $idSeq1 = $oDB->nextId( 'sequence_1' );
18         print( "idSeq1 = $idSeq1<br>" );
19
20         $oDB->disconnect();
21      }
22   ?>
```

Code Listing 9: Using Sequences

In the example, two sequences are used. The first is named 'sequence_1', the second 'sequence_2'. The output of the above code is show below in Output 3.

```
1    idSeq1 = 1
2    idSeq1 = 2
3    idSeq2 = 1
4    idSeq1 = 3
```

Output 3: Results of Sequence Example (Code Listing 9)

Before running the above code, neither sequence existed in the database. Therefore, the first value for each sequence was initially 1. If the same code is run again, the output is as shown in Output 4.

```
1    idSeq1 = 4
2    idSeq1 = 5
3    idSeq2 = 2
4    idSeq1 = 6
```

Output 4: Results of 2nd Run of Sequence Example

The implementation of sequences is database specific, but for MySQL, the implementation is achieved by creating a new table on the database called *<sequence_name>_seq* consisting of a single column, the current value of the sequence. For the above examples, two new tables were created, *sequence_1_seq* and *sequence_2_seq*.

Note that the name of the table is specified by the *seqname_format* option that can be specified during the call to **DB::connect()**. See Table 2 above for more details about this parameter. If you wish to use a different format for the sequence table, be careful to include the characters '%s' in your *seqname_format* value. See Code Listing 10 for an example of how to change the default table name format for sequence management. The **DB::connect()** call on line 5 is the relevant change.

```php
1    <?php
2      require_once( 'DB.php' );
3
4      // make a non-persistent connection to a MySQL
     database
5      $oDB = DB::connect(
     'mysql://bt_user:bt_pass@207.44.182.3/book_test',
     array( 'seqname_format' => 'seq_%s' ) );
6      if ( !DB::isError( $oDB ) )
7      {
8        $idSeq1 = $oDB->nextId( 'sequence_1' );
9        print( "idSeq1 = $idSeq1<br>" );
10
11       $idSeq1 = $oDB->nextId( 'sequence_1' );
12       print( "idSeq1 = $idSeq1<br>" );
13
14       $idSeq2 = $oDB->nextId( 'sequence_2' );
15       print( "idSeq2 = $idSeq2<br>" );
16
17       $idSeq1 = $oDB->nextId( 'sequence_1' );
18       print( "idSeq1 = $idSeq1<br>" );
19
20       $oDB->disconnect();
21     }
22   ?>
```

Code Listing 10: Custom Sequence Table name Format

As expected, running the code shown in Code Listing 10 causes two new tables to be created, *seq_sequence_1* and *seq_sequence_2*. Note that while sequences are a generalization that can make your application portable to various databases, relying on the implementation is not suggested. For example, if you rely on the table name information for sequences as implemented by the MySQL class in PEAR::DB for any purpose outside of simply using sequences, your application will not port easily to an Oracle back-end. This is due to the fact that Oracle natively supports sequences, so the tables created by the MySQL implementation will not be created by the Oracle implementation of sequences.

As a developer, I personally recommend using sequences rather than automatically incrementing field types. Depending on the underlying database, some problems can arise with automatically incrementing fields.

Prepare and Execute

The prepare and execute method of database querying is also generalized for all databases by using PEAR::DB. By using the **prepare()**, **execute()**, and **executeMultiple()** methods, more flexibility is afforded general query execution. Details of these methods will be given below, but as a high-level overview, a simple example is shown below in Code Listing 11.

```php
1   <?php
2     require_once( 'DB.php' );
3
4     // make a non-persistent connection to a MySQL
      database
5     $oDB = DB::connect(
      'mysql://bt_user:bt_pass@207.44.182.3/book_test',
      array( 'seqname_format' => 'seq_%s' ) );
6     if ( !DB::isError( $oDB ) )
7     {
8        $aInsertSQL = 'INSERT INTO Employees ( id ,
      last_name , first_name , phone_ext , mgr_id ,
      dept_id ) VALUES ( ?, ?, ?, ?, ?, ? )';
9        $hQuery    = $oDB->prepare( $aInsertSQL );
10
11       $aData  = array( $oDB->nextId( 'employees' ),
      'Schwendiman', 'Ryan', '123', '1', '1' );
12       $result = $oDB->execute( $hQuery, $aData );
13       if ( DB::isError( $result ) )
14         print( $result->getMessage() );
15
16       $aData  = array( $oDB->nextId( 'employees' ),
      'Schwendiman', 'Scott', '234', '1', '1' );
17       $result = $oDB->execute( $hQuery, $aData );
18       if ( DB::isError( $result ) )
19         print( $result->getMessage() );
20
21       $aData  = array( $oDB->nextId( 'employees' ),
      'Schwendiman', 'Taylor', '323', '1', '1' );
```

```
22        $result = $oDB->execute( $hQuery, $aData );
23        if ( DB::isError( $result ) )
24          print( $result->getMessage() );
25
26        $oDB->disconnect();
27    }
28  ?>
```

Code Listing 11: Overview of Using prepare() and execute()

To begin, queries that will use the prepare/execute model must first be parameterized such as the one shown in line 8 above. All dynamic fields are replaced by the '?' character. Next, a query handle is obtained from the database object using the **prepare()** method as shown in line 9. The handle is used later in calls to either **execute()** or **executeMultiple()**. The data that replaces the '?' fields is provided by an array parameter. Lines 11, 16 and 21 above show how to set up such an array. The parameters must be ordered in the same way as used in the prepared query. Finally, the query is executed as shown in lines 12, 17 and 22.

Developers coming from other programming/database backgrounds will recognize the prepare/execute method immediately and understand its benefits. These concepts will be discussed in detail later in the method reference for the **DB_common** class.

autoPrepare and autoExecute

autoPrepare and autoExecute are extensions of the prepare and execute mechanisms described above. The added facility is to eliminate the need for creating parameterized queries at all.

```
1   <?php
2     require_once( 'DB.php' );
3
4     $oDB = DB::connect(
    'mysql://bt_user:bt_pass@207.44.182.3/book_test',
    array( 'seqname_format' => 'seq_%s' ) );
5     if ( !DB::isError( $oDB ) )
6     {
7        $aFields    = array( 'id', 'last_name',
    'first_name', 'phone_ext', 'mgr_id', 'dept_id' );
8        $hQuery     = $oDB->autoPrepare( 'Employees',
    $aFields, DB_AUTOQUERY_INSERT );
9
10       $aData  = array( $oDB->nextId( 'employees' ),
    'Schwendiman', 'Ryan', '123', '1', '1' );
11       $result = $oDB->execute( $hQuery, $aData );
12       if ( DB::isError( $result ) )
13         print( $result->getMessage() );
14
15       $aData  = array( $oDB->nextId( 'employees' ),
    'Schwendiman', 'Scott', '234', '1', '1' );
16       $result = $oDB->execute( $hQuery, $aData );
17       if ( DB::isError( $result ) )
18         print( $result->getMessage() );
19
20       $aData  = array( $oDB->nextId( 'employees' ),
    'Schwendiman', 'Taylor', '323', '1', '1' );
21       $result = $oDB->execute( $hQuery, $aData );
22       if ( DB::isError( $result ) )
23         print( $result->getMessage() );
24
25       $oDB->disconnect();
26    }
27  ?>
```

Code Listing 12: Using autoPrepare

The example shown in Code Listing 12 illustrates the use of the **autoPrepare()** method. Rather than specifying a parameterized SQL query, as was illustrated in Code Listing 11, only the table name and field names need to be specified. The **autoPrepare()** method uses the table name, field names and a mode parameter to internally create and prepare an adequate SQL query for either INSERT or UPDATE.

The example here is simply to provide a quick overview of the **autoPrepare()** method. The **autoExecute()** method is similar and both methods will be discussed in much greater detail in the section

below for the **DB_common** class. Also, some
limitations and usage information is provided in the
discussion of the **autoExecute()** method on page 66.

Introductory Summary

This ends the introductory information to
PEAR::DB. The above high-level overview outlines
the major concepts in PEAR::DB. The following
sections detail the PEAR::DB classes and their
methods and properties.

Class DB

The main **DB** class is really just a container class
consisting of some static methods and utility
functions that are general to PEAR::DB. The static
methods listed in Table 3 are defined in the **DB** class.

Method	Description
factory()	Creates a new database connection object of a specific type. Does not actually establish a connection.
connect()	Creates a new database connection object and establishes a connection to the database server.
apiVersion()	Returns the **DB** API version.
isError()	Checks if the passed parameter is an error object.

isConnection()	Checks if the passed parameter is a DB connection type.
isWarning()	Checks if the passed parameter is a warning object.
isManip()	Checks if the passes SQL statement is a data manipulation query or a data definition query.
errorMessage()	Returns a textual error message for a numeric DB error code or DB_Error object.
parseDSN()	Returns a fully parsed DSN from a DSN string. This method is unlikely to be used directly and may normally be considered a private method.
assertExtension()	Loads a particular PHP extension dynamically as needed. This method is unlikely to be used directly and may normally be considered a private method.

Table 3: DB Class Methods

DB::factory

❖ *mixed* factory(*string* $type)

Creates a new DB connection object, but does not connect to the database server. The *type* parameter is a string value containing just the type of database object to create. Valid values are shown in the *phptype* column of Table 1 on page 19.

➲ Returns either the newly created DB object or a **DB_Error** object.

Typically this method is not used as the **connect()** method performs both DB object creation and connection. However, there may be instances where creating a DB object without a connection is preferable.

Note that if you choose to use the **factory()** method to obtain a DB object, then use the object's **connect()** method, you will need to set the options of the DB object manually. Also, you will need to call **parseDSN()** directly as the instantiated DB object expects a parsed DSN, not a DSN string. An example of this is shown in Code Listing 13.

```php
1    <?php
2      require_once( 'DB.php' );
3
4      // create an unconnected MySQL DB object
5      $oDB = DB::factory( 'mysql' );
6      if ( DB::isError( $oDB ) )
7      {
8        print( 'Unable to create MySQL DB Object<br>'
       );
9        exit;
10     }
11
12     $oDB->setOption( 'optimize', 'portability' );
13
14     $result = $oDB->connect( DB::parseDSN(
       'mysql://bt_user:bt_pass@207.44.182.3/book_test' )
       );
15     if ( DB_OK == $result )
16     {
17       // do DB work, then disconnect
18       // ...
19       $oDB->disconnect();
20     }
21     else
22     {
23       // $result is a DB_Error object
```

```
24        print( 'Unable to connect to MySQL ' . $result-
     >getMessage() . '<br>' );
25        exit;
26   }
27   ?>
```

Code Listing 13: DB::factory

In Code Listing 13, the object is created on line 5. Only the database type is specified by the call to **factory()**. The result is checked for validity, then an option is set on line 12. On line 14, the actual connection to the database server is made. Note that the DSN string passed to the **parseDSN()** method contains the database type. This is necessary for the parsing to succeed (see Code Listing 7 on page 18 for a listing of valid DSN string formats). Be sure that the database type used in the **factory()** method matches the database type specified in the DSN used to make the actual connection.

Again, it is recommended to use the **connect()** method in almost all cases.

DB::connect

❖ *mixed* connect(*mixed* $dsn, *mixed* $options = false)

This is the preferred method for creating a new database object and simultaneously connecting to a database server.

The *dsn* parameter is either a DSN string, or a parsed DSN (returned from **DB::parseDSN**). The *options* parameter may be either a Boolean value or an array. When *options* is an array, it must be an associative array whose name/value pairs can be passed to the DB object's **setOption()** method. The default options currently used are shown in Table 2 on page 20. When *options* is a Boolean value, it is interpreted to be the value of the *persistent* option which indicates whether a persistent database connection should be established.

⮑ **Returns either a valid DB connection object, or a DB_Error object.**

```php
1   <?php
2     require_once( 'DB.php' );
3
4     // make a non-persistent connection to a MySQL
      database
5     $oDB = DB::connect(
      'mysql://bt_user:bt_pass@207.44.182.3/book_test',
      false );
6     if ( !DB::isError( $oDB ) )
7     {
8       print( 'test 1 success<br>' );
9       $oDB->disconnect();
10    }
11
12    // make a persistent connection to a MySQL
      database
13    $oDB = DB::connect(
      'mysql://bt_user:bt_pass@207.44.182.3/book_test',
      true );
14    if ( !DB::isError( $oDB ) )
15    {
16      print( 'test 2 success<br>' );
17      $oDB->disconnect();
18    }
19
20    // make a persistent connection to a MySQL
      database -- alternate method
21    $oDB = DB::connect(
      'mysql://bt_user:bt_pass@207.44.182.3/book_test',
      array( 'persistent' => true ) );
22    if ( !DB::isError( $oDB ) )
23    {
24      print( 'test 3 success<br>' );
25      $oDB->disconnect();
26    }
27
28    // make a persistent connection to a MySQL
      database, set optimize to 'portability', increase
      debug level
29    $oDB = DB::connect(
      'mysql://bt_user:bt_pass@207.44.182.3/book_test',
      array( 'persistent' => true, 'optimize' =>
      'portability', 'debug' => 5 ) );
30    if ( !DB::isError( $oDB ) )
31    {
32      print( 'test 4 success<br>' );
33      $oDB->disconnect();
34    }
35
36    // same as above, but pass in parsed DSN instead
      of DSN string
```

```
37    $aDSN = DB::parseDSN(
      'mysql://bt_user:bt_pass@207.44.182.3/book_test' );
38    $oDB  = DB::connect ( $aDSN, array( 'persistent'
      => true, 'optimize' => 'portability', 'debug' => 5
      ) );
39    if ( !DB::isError( $oDB ) )
40    {
41       print( 'test 5 success<br>' );
42       $oDB->disconnect();
43    }
44  ?>
```

Code Listing 14: Several Examples of DB::connect

The **DB::connect()** examples shown in Code Listing 14 illustrate the various calling conventions.

DB::apiVersion

❖ *integer* apiVersion(*void*)

➲ Returns the DB API version. Currently the API version is 2.

DB::isError

❖ *boolean* isError(*mixed* $value)

➲ Returns true if the passed parameter, *value*, is a variable of type **DB_Error**.

DB::isConnection

❖ *boolean* isConnection(*mixed* $value)

➲ Returns true if the passed parameter, *value*, is valid DB connection class descending from **DB_common**.

DB::isWarning

❖ *boolean* isWarning(*mixed* $value)

➲ Returns true if the passed parameter, *value*, is a variable of type **DB_Warning**.

DB::isManip

❖ *boolean* isManip(*string* $query)

➲ Returns true if *query* is a data manipulation or data definition query. Currently the SQL query types that return true are: INSERT, UPDATE, DELETE, REPLACE, CREATE, DROP, ALTER, GRANT, REVOKE, LOCK and UNLOCK.

DB::errorMessage

❖ *string* errorMessage(*mixed* $value)

➲ Returns the text description of the error represented by *value*.

The *value* parameter may be either a numeric error code or an object of type **DB_Error**.

DB::parseDSN

❖ *array* parseDSN(*mixed* $dsn)

The *dsn* parameter may be either an array or a string. If it is an array, it is assumed to be a pre-parsed DSN and is simply returned to the caller. Otherwise, the string is parsed.

➲ Returns an associative array consisting o f the elements shown in Table 4.

Element	Default Value	Description
phptype	false	Database backend used in PHP (mysql, odbc etc.)

dbsyntax	false	Database used with regards to SQL syntax etc.
username	false	User name for login
password	false	Password for login
protocol	false	Communication protocol to use (tcp, unix etc.)
hostspec	false	Host specification (hostname[:port])
port	false	Port on which to connect
socket	false	Socket on which to connect
database	false	Database to use on the DBMS server

Table 4: DSN Array Elements

Each back-end database server may use the DSN elements differently. For examples of valid DSNs for each database server, see the sections below that detail specifically the database servers.

DB::assertExtension

❖ *boolean* assertExtension(*string* $name)

Loads a PHP extension based on the *name* parameter passed in. For the purposes of PEAR::DB, the extensions are the database extensions (e.g. mysql, oci8, etc.).

➲ Returns true if the extension is loaded.

```
1  <?php
2    require_once( 'DB.php' );
3
4    $aExtensions = array( 'mysql', 'pgsql', 'ibase',
   'msql', 'mssql', 'oci8', 'odbc', 'sybase', 'ifx',
   'fbsql', 'sqlite', 'dbase' );
5
6    foreach( $aExtensions as $aExt )
```

```
7     {
8        if ( DB::assertExtension( $aExt ) )
9           print( $aExt . ' extension loaded<br>' );
10       else
11          print( $aExt . ' extension not loaded<br>' );
12    }
13  ?>
```

Code Listing 15: DB::assertExtension Example

The example code shown in Code Listing 15 illustrates how to check for each of the supported PEAR::DB database servers. The output for my Windows-based installation is shown in Output 5.

```
1    mysql extension loaded
2    pgsql extension not loaded
3    ibase extension not loaded
4    msql extension not loaded
5    mssql extension not loaded
6    oci8 extension not loaded
7    odbc extension loaded
8    sybase extension not loaded
9    ifx extension not loaded
10   fbsql extension not loaded
11   sqlite extension not loaded
12   dbase extension not loaded
```

Output 5: DB::assertExtension Example Output

Class DB Summary

Only two members of the **DB** class are commonly used in an average development project, **connect** and **isError**. The other methods are helpful in certain circumstances, but will be rarely used. Typically the **DB** class methods will be used statically; there is no need to create an object of type **DB**.

Class DB_common

Class **DB_common** is the parent class of all of the database-server specific classes. The purpose of **DB_common** is to provide a common interface definition for all the concrete implementation classes. **DB_common** can be thought of, in a way, as an abstract base class since many of the methods defined in **DB_common** do nothing but return an error.

The methods described in this section are the common methods available to all database server classes.

Method	Description
toString()	String conversion. This method provides a string representation of the DB_common object.
quoteString()	Quotes a string so it can be safely used within string delimiters in a query (preserved for compatibility issues, quote() is preferred).
quote()	Preferred method for quoting a string for safe use within queries.
provides()	Tell whether a DB implementation or its backend extension supports a given feature.
errorCode()	Map native error codes to portable PEAR::DB codes.
errorMessage()	Map a DB error code to a textual message. This is actually just a wrapper

	for DB::errorMessage().
raiseError()	This method is used to communicate an error and invoke error callbacks etc. A wrapper for PEAR::raiseError.
setFetchMode()	Sets which fetch mode should be used by default for queries on this connection.
setOption()	Set the option for the db class.
getOption()	Returns the value of an option.
prepare()	Prepares a query for multiple execution with execute(). With some database back ends, this is emulated.
autoPrepare()	Automatically create an INSERT or UPDATE query and then call prepare().
autoExecute()	Automatically create an INSERT or UPDATE query and then call prepare() and execute().
buildManipSQL	Create a SQL query for the prepare() method.
execute()	Executes a prepared SQL query.
executeEmulateQuery()	Emulates the execute statement, when not supported prepare/execute.
executeMultiple()	This function does

	several execute() calls on the same statement handle.
freePrepared()	Free the resources allocated in a prepare()'ed query.
modifyQuery()	This method is used by back ends to alter queries for various reasons. It is defined here to assure that all implementations have this method defined.
modifyLimitQuery()	This method is used by back ends to alter limited queries.
query()	Send a query to the database and return any results with a DB_result object.
limitQuery()	Generates a limited query (experimental).
getOne()	Fetch the first column of the first row of data returned from a query. Performs the query and frees the results.
getRow()	Fetch the first row of data returned from a query. Performs the query and frees the results.
getCol()	Fetch a single column from a result set and return it as an indexed array.

getAssoc()	Fetch the entire result set of a query and return it as an associative array using the first column as the key. If the result set contains more than two columns, the value is an array of the values from column 2-n. If the result set contains only two columns, the returned value will be a scalar with the value of the second column (unless forced to an array with the $force_array parameter).
getAll()	Fetch all the rows returned from a query.
autoCommit()	Enable automatic commit.
commit()	Starts a commit.
rollback()	Starts a rollback.
numRows()	Returns the number of rows in a result object.
affectedRows()	Returns the affected rows of a query.
errorNative()	Returns an error message, provided by the database.
nextId()	Returns the next free id of a sequence.
createSequence()	Creates a new sequence.
dropSequence()	Deletes a sequence.
tableInfo()	Returns meta data about the result set.

getTables()	List tables in a database.
getListOf()	List internal DB info.
getSequenceName()	Returns a properly-formatted sequence table name for a sequence.

DB_common::toString

❖ *string* toString(*void*)

The **toString()** method is an internal method that is not expected to be used externally. Its documentation lists its access as private. For curiosity, an example and its output are shown in Code Listing 16 and Output 6, respectively.

```
13  <?php
14    require_once( 'DB.php' );
15
16    $oDB = DB::connect(
   'mysql://bt_user:bt_pass@207.44.182.3/book_test',
   false );
17    if ( !DB::isError( $oDB ) )
18    {
19      print( $oDB->toString() . '<br>' );
20      $oDB->disconnect();
21    }
22  ?>
```

Code Listing 16: DB_common::toString Example

```
1   db_mysql: (phptype=mysql, dbsyntax=mysql)
    [connected]
```

Output 6: DB_common::toString Output

DB_common::quoteString

❖ *string* quoteString(*string* $string)

The **quoteString()** method is available for compatibility reasons, but programmers are encouraged to use the **quote()** method.

DB_common::quote

❖ *string* quote (*string* $string)

➲ Returns a quoted string so it can be safely used in a query.

The **quote()** method safely quotes and escapes values based on the requirements of the particular back end database. The example code in Code Listing 17 illustrates the **quote()** method and the output in Output 7 shows how the various DB objects may provide different results.

```php
1    <?php
2      require_once( 'DB.php' );
3
4      print( 'Quoting with mysql object<br>' );
5      $oDB = DB::connect(
     'mysql://bt_user:bt_pass@207.44.182.3/book_test',
     false );
6      if ( !DB::isError( $oDB ) )
7      {
8        print( $oDB->quote( ) . '<br>' );
9        print( $oDB->quote( 500 ) . '<br>' );
10       print( $oDB->quote( 'some text' ) . '<br>' );
11       print( $oDB->quote( "it's not on drive c:\
     anywhere" ) . '<br>' );
12       $oDB->disconnect();
13     }
14     print( '<br><br>Quoting with ODBC object<br>' );
15     $oDB = DB::connect( 'odbc://book_test', true );
16     if ( !DB::isError( $oDB ) )
17     {
18       print( $oDB->quote( ) . '<br>' );
19       print( $oDB->quote( 500 ) . '<br>' );
20       print( $oDB->quote( 'some text' ) . '<br>' );
21       print( $oDB->quote( "it's not on drive c:\
     anywhere" ) . '<br>' );
22       $oDB->disconnect();
23     }
24   ?>
```

Code Listing 17: DB_common::quote Example

```
1   Quoting with mysql object
2   NULL
3   500
4   'some text'
5   'it\'s not on drive c:\\ anywhere'
6
7
8   Quoting with ODBC object
9   NULL
10  500
11  'some text'
12  'it''s not on drive c:\ anywhere'
```

Output 7: DB_common::quote Example Output

DB_common::provides

❖ *mixed* provides(*string* $feature)

➲ Returns whether this DB implementation supports *feature*.

There are currently four defined features: *prepare*, *pconnect*, *transactions* and *limit*. This method is primarily used internally to determine what types of requests are possible given the particular database object.

The sample shown in Code Listing 18 displays a table containing all of the features and their values for all database types. The output has been reformatted for this book and is shown in Table 5.

```php
1   <?php
2     require_once( 'DB.php' );
3
4     $aPHPTypes = array( 'mysql', 'pgsql', 'ibase',
    'msql', 'mssql', 'oci8', 'odbc', 'sybase', 'ifx',
    'fbsql', 'sqlite', 'dbase' );
5     $aFeatures = array( 'prepare', 'pconnect',
    'transactions', 'limit' );
6
7     print( '<table><tr>' );
8     print( '<td> </td>' );
9
10    foreach( $aFeatures as $aFeature )
11      print( '<td>' . $aFeature . '</td>' );
12
```

```
13    print( '</tr>' );
14
15    foreach ( $aPHPTypes as $aType )
16    {
17      $oDB = DB::factory( $aType );
18      if ( !DB::isError( $oDB ) )
19      {
20        print( '<tr><td>' . $aType . '</td>' );
21        foreach( $aFeatures as $aFeature )
22        {
23          $result = $oDB->provides( $aFeature );
24          if ( gettype( $result ) == 'boolean' )
25            print( '<td>' . ( $oDB->provides(
   $aFeature ) ? 'true' : 'false' ) . '</td>' );
26          else
27            print( '<td>' . $oDB->provides( $aFeature
   ) . '</td>' );
28        }
29
30        print( '</tr>' );
31      }
32    }
33  ?>
```

Code Listing 18: DB_common::provides Example

	prepare	pconnect	transactions	limit
mysql	false	true	true	alter
pgsql	false	true	true	alter
ibase	true	true	true	false
msql	false	true	false	emulate
mssql	false	true	true	emulate
oci8	false	true	true	alter
odbc	true	true	false	emulate
sybase	false	true	false	emulate
ifx	false	true	true	emulate
fbsql	false	true	true	emulate
sqlite	false	true	true	alter

dbase	false	false	false	false

Table 5: Results of Code Listing 18 (re-formatted for book)

DB_common::errorCode

❖ *int* errorCode(*mixed* $nativecode)

The **errorCode()** method converts a native DB error code to a PEAR::DB portable error code. This may be used in conjunction with the **errorNative()** method described in this section. The *nativecode* parameter may be a string or an integer.

➲ Returns a portable DB error code.

```
<?php
  require_once( 'DB.php' );

  $oDB = DB::connect(
  'mysql://bt_user:bt_pass@207.44.182.3/book_test',
  false );
  if ( !DB::isError( $oDB ) )
  {
    $sSQL = 'select * from bogus_table'; // table,
  bogus_table, does not exist
    $oRows = $oDB->query( $sSQL );

    // you can use error codes
    $aErrCode = $oDB->errorNative();
    $aPEARCode = $oDB->errorCode( $aErrCode );
    print( "Native Error Code = $aErrCode<br>" );
    print( "PEAR Error Code = $aPEARCode<br>" );
    print( '<br>' );
    print( 'Native Error Message: ' . mysql_error()
  . '<br>' );
    print( 'PEAR Error Message: ' . $oDB-
  >errorMessage( $aErrCode ) . '<br>' );

    print( '<br>' );
    // but if there's an error, a DB_Error object
  provides great information
    if ( DB::isError( $oRows ) )
    {
      print( 'Error Message: ' . $oRows->message .
  '<br>' );
      print( 'User Info: ' . $oRows->userinfo .
  '<br>' );
    }

    $oDB->disconnect();
  }
```

```
29
30   ?>
```

**Code Listing 19: DB_common::errorCode,
DB_common::errorMessage, DB_common::errorNative()
Example**

The example in Code Listing 19 illustrates usage of
the **errorCode()** method. For some types of error
handling, the PEAR::DB error code or the native
database error code may provide valuable
information. For example, you may want to test if the
current user has some type of permissions. By
checking the actual error codes, the program can
continue providing the right user experience.

For many error conditions, however, the **DB_Error**
object returned by most PEAR::DB methods
provides the right level of detail such that the error
codes are simply redundant information.

DB_common::errorMessage

❖ *string* errorMessage(*integer* $dbcode)

➲ Returns a textual error message based on the *dbcode*
parameter which must be a native database engine
error code.

An example of usage is show in Code Listing 19 on
page 47.

DB_common::raiseError

❖ *object* raiseError(*mixed* $code = DB_ERROR, *int*
$mode = null, *mixed* $options = null, *string*
$userinfo = null, *mixed* $native = null)

This method is used to communicate an error and invoke error callbacks etc. It is basically a wrapper for PEAR::raiseError without the message string.

The **raiseError()** method is mostly used internally, but you may wish to use it in your programs. For more information about this method, investigate the PEAR::raiseError method.

The *code* parameter is an integer error code or a PEAR error object. If an object, all other parameters are ignored. The *mode* and *options* parameters are specific to the PEAR::raiseError implementation and are not discussed here. The *userinfo* and *native* parameters are used to represent the database specific error message and native error code, respectively.

➲ Returns a PEAR error object.

Most of the examples in this book show generally how to use the **DB_Error** object as it is returned. In most production environments, only the very basic information about failures will likely be displayed. However, for development, it is handy to have detailed information displayed in the event of an error.

In fact, the **DB_Error** object contains so much information that it's hard not to be compelled to use it in all cases. The example shown in Code Listing 20 illustrates how to use the **DB_Error** object to provide detailed information about errors. The script may be a little hard to read because it's a PHP script that generates a Javascript script on the fly, but its effect is very cool. Whenever the **errorPopup** function is called, a new popup window is displayed containing detailed error information. This is nice because it

Comprehensive PHP PEAR::DB

doesn't pollute the main display window with error information. An example of the popup window is shown in Figure 4 on page 52.

```
1    <!DOCTYPE HTML PUBLIC "-//W3C//DTD HTML 4.0
     Transitional//EN">
2
3    <html>
4    <head>
5            <title>Untitled</title>
6    </head>
7
8    <body>
9
10   <?php
11     require_once( 'DB.php' );
12
13     function formatArg( $aArgument )
14     {
15       switch ( gettype( $aArgument ) )
16       {
17         case 'boolean'  : return ( $aArgument ?
     'true' : 'false' );
18         case 'integer'  :
19         case 'double'   : return $aArgument;
20         case 'string'   : return '"' . $aArgument .
     '"';
21         case 'array'    : return '[array]';
22         case 'object'   : return '[object]';
23         case 'resource' : return '[resource]';
24         case 'NULL'     : return 'null';
25       }
26     }
27
28     function formatArgs( $aArguments )
29     {
30       if ( count( $aArguments ) == 0 )
31         return '';
32
33       $nCount = 0;
34       $result = '';
35       foreach ( $aArguments as $aArgument )
36       {
37         if ( $nCount != 0 )
38           $result .= ', ';
39
40         $result .= formatArg( $aArgument );
41
42         $nCount++;
43       }
44
45       return $result;
46     }
47
48     function formatBacktraceElem( $aElement )
49     {
50       $result = '';
51
52       $result .= '&middot; Line ' . $aElement['line']
     . ' of ';
```

Page 49

```
53      $result .= str_replace( '\\', '\\\\',
    $aElement['file'] ) . '<ul>';
54
55      $result .= $aElement['class'] .
    $aElement['type'] . $aElement['function'];
56      $result .= '( ' . formatArgs( $aElement['args']
    ) . ' )</ul>';
57
58      return $result;
59    }
60
61    function errorPopup( $dbError )
62    {
63      // just to be safe, make sure the parameter is
    a DB_Error
64      if ( DB::isError( $dbError ) )
65      {
66        $output  = '<table>';
67        $output .= '  <tr>';
68        $output .= '    <td>';
69        $output .= '      Error Message: ';
70        $output .= '    </td>';
71        $output .= '    <td>';
72        $output .= '      ' . $dbError->message;
73        $output .= '    </td>';
74        $output .= '  </tr>';
75        $output .= '  <tr>';
76        $output .= '    <td>';
77        $output .= '      User Information: ';
78        $output .= '    </td>';
79        $output .= '    <td>';
80        $output .= '      ' . $dbError->userinfo;
81        $output .= '    </td>';
82        $output .= '  </tr>';
83        $output .= '</table>';
84        $output .= '<br><br>';
85        $output .= '<p>Stack Trace</p>';
86        $output .= '<table>';
87
88        if ( count( $dbError->backtrace ) > 0 )
89        {
90          foreach ( $dbError->backtrace as $aElement
    )
91          {
92            $output .= '  <tr>';
93            $output .= '    <td>';
94            $output .= formatBacktraceElem( $aElement
    );
95            $output .= '    </td>';
96            $output .= '  </tr>';
97          }
98        }
99
100       $output .= '</table>';
101
102       print( '  <script>' ); print( "\n" );
103       print( '  <!--' ); print( "\n" );
104       print( '    debugWin = window.open(
    "about:blank", "", "width=600, height=300,
    staus=no, location=no, resizable=yes,
    scrollbars=yes" );' ); print( "\n" );
```

```
105      print( '    debugWin.document.write(
\'<!DOCTYPE HTML PUBLIC "-//W3C//DTD HTML 4.01
Transitional//EN">\' );' ); print( "\n" );
106      print( '    debugWin.document.write(
\'<html>\' );' ); print( "\n" );
107      print( '    debugWin.document.write(
\'<head>\' );' ); print( "\n" );
108      print( '    debugWin.document.write( \'
<title>Debug Output</title>\' );' ); print( "\n" );
109      print( '    debugWin.document.write( \'
<style type="text/css"><!-- \' );' ); print( "\n"
);
110      print( '    debugWin.document.write( \'TD {\'
);' ); print( "\n" );
111      print( '    debugWin.document.write( \' font
: normal 11px Verdana;\' );' ); print( "\n" );
112      print( '    debugWin.document.write( \'
vertical-align : top;\' );' ); print( "\n" );
113      print( '    debugWin.document.write( \'}\'
);' ); print( "\n" );
114      print( '    debugWin.document.write( \'P {\'
);' ); print( "\n" );
115      print( '    debugWin.document.write( \' font
: normal 11px Verdana;\' );' ); print( "\n" );
116      print( '    debugWin.document.write( \'}\'
);' ); print( "\n" );
117      print( '    debugWin.document.write( \'UL {\'
);' ); print( "\n" );
118      print( '    debugWin.document.write( \' font
: normal 11px Verdana;\' );' ); print( "\n" );
119      print( '    debugWin.document.write( \'}\'
);' ); print( "\n" );
120      print( '    debugWin.document.write( \'-->\'
);' ); print( "\n" );
121      print( '    debugWin.document.write(
\'</style>\' );' ); print( "\n" );
122      print( '    debugWin.document.write(
\'</head>\' );' ); print( "\n" );
123      print( '    debugWin.document.write(
\'<body>\' );' ); print( "\n" );
124      print( '    debugWin.document.write( \'<p>\'
);' ); print( "\n" );
125      print( '    debugWin.document.write( \'</p>\'
);' ); print( "\n" );
126      print( '    debugWin.document.write( \'<p>' .
str_replace( "'", "\'", $output ) . '</p>\' );' );
print( "\n" );
127      print( '    debugWin.document.write(
\'</body>\' );' ); print( "\n" );
128      print( '    debugWin.document.write(
\'</html>\' );' ); print( "\n" );
129      print( '  //-->' ); print( "\n" );
130      print( '</script>' ); print( "\n" );
131    }
132  }
133
134  $oDB = DB::connect(
  'mysql://bt_user:wrongpass@207.44.182.3/book_test',
  false );
135  if ( DB::isError( $oDB ) )
136  {
137    errorPopup( $oDB );
138  }
```

```
139
140  ?>
141
142  </body>
143  </html>
```

Code Listing 20: Using DB_Error

Figure 4: Popup window created by errorPopup function

DB_common::setFetchMode

❖ *void* setFetchMode(*integer* $fetchmode, *string*
  $object_class = null)

Sets which fetch mode should be used by default on
queries on this connection. Valid values for the
fetchmode parameter are

DB_FETCHMODE_ORDERED,
DB_FETCHMODE_ASSOC (possibly bit-wise
OR'ed with DB_FETCHMODE_FLIPPED) and
DB_FETCHMODE_OBJECT. If *fetchmode* is
DB_FETCHMODE_OBJECT, then *object_class*
specifies the class of the object to be returned by the
fetch methods. If DB_FETCHMODE_OBJECT is
used and *object_class* is null, a default cast to object
from the associative array will be done.

The default *fetchmode* is
DB_FETCHMODE_ORDERED. The example in
Code Listing 21 illustrates this.

```php
<?php
  require_once( 'DB.php' );

  $oDB = DB::connect(
'mysql://bt_user:bt_pass@207.44.182.3/book_test',
false );
  if ( DB::isConnection( $oDB ) )
  {
    $sSQL = 'select id, first_name, last_name from
Employees limit 3';
    $oRows = $oDB->query( $sSQL );

    if ( !DB::isError( $oRows ) )
    {
      while ( $aData = $oRows->fetchRow() )
      {
        print( '<pre>' );
        print_r( $aData );
        print( '</pre><br><br>' );
      }
    }

    $oDB->disconnect();
  }
?>
```

**Code Listing 21: DB_common::setFetchMode –
DB_FETCHMODE_ORDERED (default)**

The output of Code Listing 21 is shown in Output 8.

```
Array
(
    [0] => 1
    [1] => Blake
```

```
 5          [2] => Schwendiman
 6    )
 7
 8    Array
 9    (
10          [0] => 2
11          [1] => Jeffrey
12          [2] => Cox
13    )
14
15    Array
16    (
17          [0] => 3
18          [1] => Kate
19          [2] => McNulty
20    )
```

Output 8: Output when setFetchMode is DB_FETCHMODE_ORDERED

As can be seen from the printed information in Output 8, each call to DB_result::fetchRow() with the *fetchmode* set to DB_FETCHMODE_ORDERED results in an indexed array in which the indexes represent column numbers in the result dataset. The columns are ordered in the same way as the original SELECT query.

The code in Code Listing 22 and the output in Output 9 illustrate the effects of using the DB_FETCHMODE_ASSOC *fetchmode*.

```php
 1  <?php
 2    require_once( 'DB.php' );
 3
 4    $oDB = DB::connect(
       'mysql://bt_user:bt_pass@207.44.182.3/book_test',
       false );
 5    if ( DB::isConnection( $oDB ) )
 6    {
 7      $oDB->setFetchMode( DB_FETCHMODE_ASSOC );
 8
 9      $sSQL  = 'select id, first_name, last_name from
       Employees limit 3';
10      $oRows = $oDB->query( $sSQL );
11
12      if ( !DB::isError( $oRows ) )
13      {
14        while ( $aData = $oRows->fetchRow() )
15        {
16          print( '<pre>' );
17          print_r( $aData );
```

```
18              print( '</pre>' );
19          }
20      }
21
22      $oDB->disconnect();
23  }
24  ?>
```

**Code Listing 22: DB_common::setFetchMode –
DB_FETCHMODE_ASSOC**

```
1   Array
2   (
3       [id] => 1
4       [first_name] => Blake
5       [last_name] => Schwendiman
6   )
7   Array
8   (
9       [id] => 2
10      [first_name] => Jeffrey
11      [last_name] => Cox
12  )
13  Array
14  (
15      [id] => 3
16      [first_name] => Kate
17      [last_name] => McNulty
18  )
```

**Output 9: Output when setFetchMode is
DB_FETCHMODE_ASSOC**

The DB_FETCHMODE_ASSOC *fetchmode* causes
the result array to be an associative array where the
keys are the column names. Typically this is the
preferred development method because the code
itself becomes easier to read and therefore easier to
maintain.

The DB_FETCHMODE_OJBECT *fetchmode* is very
similar to the DB_FETCHMODE_ASSOC *fetchmode*.
However, instead of each result being an associative
array, each result is an object whose properties are the
names of the columns. When using
DB_FETCHMODE_OBJECT, the second
parameter of the setFetchMode() function is available

to specify an object class (*object_class*). If no *object_class* is specified, then the result object is of type **stdClass**, the default PHP object type.

```
1   <?php
2     require_once( 'DB.php' );
3
4     $oDB = DB::connect(
      'mysql://bt_user:bt_pass@207.44.182.3/book_test',
      false );
5     if ( DB::isConnection( $oDB ) )
6     {
7        $oDB->setFetchMode( DB_FETCHMODE_OBJECT );
8
9        $sSQL  = 'select id, first_name, last_name from
      Employees limit 3';
10       $oRows = $oDB->query( $sSQL );
11
12       if ( !DB::isError( $oRows ) )
13       {
14         while ( $aData = $oRows->fetchRow() )
15         {
16           print( '<pre>' );
17           print_r( $aData );
18           print( '</pre>' );
19         }
20       }
21
22       $oDB->disconnect();
23     }
24  ?>
```

Code Listing 23: DB_common::setFetchMode – DB_FETCHMODE_OBJECT

```
1   stdClass Object
2   (
3       [id] => 1
4       [first_name] => Blake
5       [last_name] => Schwendiman
6   )
7   stdClass Object
8   (
9       [id] => 2
10      [first_name] => Jeffrey
11      [last_name] => Cox
12  )
13  stdClass Object
14  (
15      [id] => 3
16      [first_name] => Kate
17      [last_name] => McNulty
18  )
```

Output 10: Output when setFetchMode is DB_FETCHMODE_OBJECT

As can be seen from Code Listing 23 and its output in Output 10, the result of using DB_FETCHMODE_OBJECT is that each call to fetchRow() returns an object. When no *object_class* is specified, as above, the resulting object is simply PHP's default cast from an array to an object.

If you plan to use the DB_FETCHMODE_OJBECT *fetchmode*, it is likely that you are developing an object-oriented application in which you may plan to use OO objects to represent database data generally. If so, your data objects will likely need to be more complex than the simple **stdClass** object.

If you wish to implement such a scenario, you can specify the *object_class* in the setFetchMode() method as shown in Code Listing 24 and Output 11.

```php
1    <?php
2      require_once( 'DB.php' );
3
4      class Employee
5      {
6        var $first_name;
7        var $last_name;
8        var $id;
9        var $full_name;
10
11        // constructor is called by DB class with a
      data row array
12        function Employee( &$arr )
13        {
14          $this->first_name = $arr['first_name'];
15          $this->last_name  = $arr['last_name'];
16          $this->id         = $arr['id'];
17
18          $this->full_name = $this->first_name . ' ' .
      $this->last_name;
19        }
20      }
21
22      $oDB = DB::connect(
      'mysql://bt_user:bt_pass@207.44.182.3/book_test',
      false );
23      if ( DB::isConnection( $oDB ) )
24      {
25        $oDB->setFetchMode( DB_FETCHMODE_OBJECT );
26
```

```
27    $sSQL  = 'select id, first_name, last_name from
Employees limit 3';
28    $oRows = $oDB->query( $sSQL, 'Employee' );
29
30    if ( !DB::isError( $oRows ) )
31    {
32      while ( $aData = $oRows->fetchRow() )
33      {
34        print( '<pre>' );
35        print_r( $aData );
36        print( '</pre>' );
37      }
38    }
39
40    $oDB->disconnect();
41  }
42  ?>
```

Code Listing 24: DB_common::setFetchMode –
DB_FETCHMODE_OBJECT using *object_class*
parameter

```
1   employee Object
2   (
3       [first_name] => Blake
4       [last_name] => Schwendiman
5       [id] => 1
6       [full_name] => Blake Schwendiman
7   )
8   employee Object
9   (
10      [first_name] => Jeffrey
11      [last_name] => Cox
12      [id] => 2
13      [full_name] => Jeffrey Cox
14  )
15  employee Object
16  (
17      [first_name] => Kate
18      [last_name] => McNulty
19      [id] => 3
20      [full_name] => Kate McNulty
21  )
```

Output 11: Output when setFetchMode is
DB_FETCHMODE_OBJECT and *object_class* is set

While the example shown in Code Listing 24 is
obviously a simple contrived example, it illustrates the
fundamental power of using
DB_FETCHMODE_OBJECT. The constructor of
the *object_class* could perform any additional work
required to instantiate an object representing the

underlying data. Depending on your needs, this mechanism may provide the skeleton for a powerful OO solution. If you are interested in OO data objects, you should also consider the information in the section describing **Class DB_storage** (page 122).

The last option to be discussed for setFetchMode() is DB_FETCHMODE_FLIPPED. While the internal code documentation claims that setFetchMode() globally affects the way that data is retrieved, in practice, this is not completely accurate. The DB_FETCHMODE_FLIPPED option is only used DB_common::getAll() method and if it is to be used, it must be passed into the method at call time. Therefore the DB_FETCHMODE_FLIPPED option will be discussed in the section for DB_common::getAll on page 90.

DB_common::setOption

❖ *mixed* setOption(*string* $option, *mixed* $value)

Sets an option for the object. The available options are shown in Table 2 on page 20. Only options named in that table can be set or retrieved.

➲ Returns DB_OK or DB_Error if the *option* parameter is not one of the valid options.

See Code Listing 13 on page 32 for a usage example.

DB_common::getOption

❖ *mixed* getOption(*string* $option)

Returns the value of an option from the object. The available options are shown in Table 2 on page 20.

Only options named in that table can be set or retrieved.

⊃ Returns the value of the *option* or DB_Error if the *option* parameter is not one of the valid options.

See Code Listing 13 on page 32 for a usage example.

DB_common::prepare

❖ *resource* prepare(*string* $query)

The **prepare()** method prepares a specially-formatted query string for use in the prepare/execute methodology of querying. Typically this is used when multiple similar queries will be run simultaneously.

The *query* parameter is specially formatted to include placeholder characters that will represent real data when the **execute()** method is called. The placeholder characters and their meanings are shown in Table 6.

Placeholder Character	Definition
?	A quoted scalar value such as a string or integer.
&	Replaced data must be a file name. The contents of the file will be the actual data.
!	Scalar value inserted AS IS.

Table 6: Placeholder characters for use in query() method

The example shown in Code Listing 25 illustrates how the **prepare()** statement can be used to facilitate inserting several similar rows of data into the *Paychecks*

table described in the examples earlier (see Code
Listing 1 on page 10).

```
1   <?php
2     require_once( 'DB.php' );
3
4     $oDB = DB::connect(
      'mysql://bt_user:bt_pass@207.44.182.3/book_test',
      true );
5     if ( DB::isConnection( $oDB ) )
6     {
7       $sSQL = 'insert into Paychecks ( employee_id,
      check_date, check_number,
8     gross_pay, benefits_withheld, taxes_withheld )
      values ( ?, !, ?, ?, ?, ? )';
9
10      $hQuery = $oDB->prepare( $sSQL );
11
12      $oDB->execute( $hQuery, array( 1, 'NOW()', 123,
      1098.65, 124.55, 98.98 ) );
13      $oDB->execute( $hQuery, array( 2, 'NOW()', 123,
      1198.65, 124.55, 99.98 ) );
14      $oDB->execute( $hQuery, array( 3, 'NOW()', 123,
      1298.65, 124.55, 95.98 ) );
15
16      $oDB->freePrepared( $hQuery );
17      $oDB->disconnect();
18    }
19  ?>
```

Code Listing 25: Using prepare() -- simple example

The example shown in Code Listing 25 illustrates the
use of two of the placeholder characters, '?' and '!'.
The important difference in this example is that the
second placeholder (the '!') is used because the data is
a MySQL function, **NOW()**, which specifies the date
that the query runs on the server. If the '?'
placeholder had been used, the interpretation of the
query would have been to try to insert the literal
string, 'NOW()' into the database. In most cases, the
'?' placeholder is the most appropriate, but there are
times when the '!' placeholder is the only one that will
achieve the desired results.

To illustrate the use of the '&' placeholder, a much
more complex example is required. The SQL

statements in Code Listing 26 show the definition of the table that will be used in this example.

```
1   CREATE TABLE `UploadedFiles` (
2   `id` INT NOT NULL AUTO_INCREMENT ,
    `filename` VARCHAR( 250 ) NOT NULL ,
    `filesize` INT NOT NULL ,
    `enctype` VARCHAR( 50 ) NOT NULL ,
    `filedata` BLOB NOT NULL ,
    PRIMARY KEY ( `id` )
3   );
```

Code Listing 26: SQL Statements for Creating the UploadedFiles Table

The example in Code Listing 27 shows how to create a very simple form for uploading a file and storing its contents in a MySQL database.

```
1   <?php
2     if ( $_SERVER['REQUEST_METHOD'] == 'POST' )
3     {
4       if ( is_uploaded_file(
    $_FILES['upload_file']['tmp_name'] ) )
5       {
6         require_once( 'DB.php' );
7
8         $oDB = DB::connect(
    'mysql://bt_user:bt_pass@207.44.182.3/book_test',
    true );
9         if ( DB::isConnection( $oDB ) )
10        {
11          $sSQL = 'insert into UploadedFiles (
    filename, filesize, filedata, enctype ) values ( ?,
    ?, &, ? )';
12
13          $hQuery = $oDB->prepare( $sSQL );
14
15          $oDB->execute( $hQuery, array(
    $_FILES['upload_file']['name'],
    $_FILES['upload_file']['size'],
    $_FILES['upload_file']['tmp_name'],
16  $_FILES['upload_file']['type'] ) );
17
18          $oDB->freePrepared( $hQuery );
19          $oDB->disconnect();
20        }
21      }
22    }
23  ?>
24  <html>
25  <body>
26  <form action="<?php print( $_SERVER['SCRIPT_NAME']
    ); ?>" method="POST" enctype="multipart/form-data">
```

```
27    File to upload: <input type="File"
   name="upload_file"><br>
28          <input type="Submit" value="Submit">
29  </form>
30  </body>
31  </html>
```

**Code Listing 27: The prepare() method using the '&'
placeholder**

The example shown Code Listing 27 requires a basic
understanding of the process of file uploading in PHP
which can be found at
**http://www.php.net/manual/en/features.file-
upload.php**. The basic concept is that when a file is
uploaded, the superglobal **$_FILES** contains
information about the uploaded files that can be used.
In this case, the uploaded file is checked for validity
on line 4. If this passes, a simple database query is
prepared using the '&' placeholder. Then the query is
executed such that the value for the '&' placeholder is
the full path to the temporary file containing the
uploaded file contents. By doing so, the entire
contents of the uploaded file are stored into the
database.

➲ Returns a handle to a prepared query that can be used
by the **execute()** and similar methods.

DB_common::autoPrepare

❖ *resource* autoPrepare(*string* $table, *array*
$table_fields, *int* $mode = DB_AUTOQUERY_INSERT,
mixed $where = false)

The **autoPrepare()** method is similar to the
prepare() method in that it returns a handle that can
be used by **execute()**, but differs in that it takes
arguments that first build the parameterized query.

This eliminates the need for you to specify the parameterized query at all.

The code in Code Listing 28 shows usage.

```
1    <?php
2      require_once( 'DB.php' );
3
4      $oDB = DB::connect(
       'mysql://bt_user:bt_pass@207.44.182.3/book_test',
       true );
5      if ( DB::isConnection( $oDB ) )
6      {
7        $hQuery = $oDB->autoPrepare( 'Paychecks',
       array( 'employee_id', 'check_date', 'check_number',
       'gross_pay', 'benefits_withheld', 'taxes_withheld'
       ) );
8
9        $oDB->execute( $hQuery, array( 1, '2003-11-26',
       124, 1098.65, 124.55, 98.98 ) );
10       $oDB->execute( $hQuery, array( 2, '2003-11-26',
       124, 1198.65, 124.55, 99.98 ) );
11       $oDB->execute( $hQuery, array( 3, '2003-11-26',
       124, 1298.65, 124.55, 95.98 ) );
12
13       $oDB->freePrepared( $hQuery );
14       $oDB->disconnect();
15     }
16   ?>
```

Code Listing 28: Using autoPrepare() – INSERT

The code in Code Listing 28 is identical in function to the code in Code Listing 25. Rather than specifying a parameterized query, using **autoPrepare()** allows you to specify just the table, fields and type of query. PEAR::DB then creates the correctly formatted query on the fly and passes it on to **prepare()**. To see an example of the actual query that is built, check the examples for the **buildManipSQL()** method on page 67.

One important difference between Code Listing 25 and Code Listing 28 is that in the former listing, the '!' parameter type was used to allow the use of the MySQL **NOW()** function within the **execute()** method. When using **autoPrepare()**, all parameters are assumed to be the '?' type and therefore the values passed to **execute()** must be literal values to be stored in the database.

The example in Code Listing 28 shows how to automatically prepare an INSERT query. Code Listing 29 shows how to use **autoPrepare()** to effect an UPDATE.

```
1   <?php
2     require_once( 'DB.php' );
3
4     $oDB = DB::connect(
      'mysql://bt_user:bt_pass@207.44.182.3/book_test',
      true );
5     if ( DB::isConnection( $oDB ) )
6     {
7         $hQuery = $oDB->autoPrepare( 'Paychecks',
      array( 'employee_id', 'check_date', 'check_number',
      'gross_pay', 'benefits_withheld', 'taxes_withheld'
      ),
8   DB_AUTOQUERY_UPDATE, 'check_number = 124' );
9
10        $oDB->execute( $hQuery, array( 1, '2003-11-26',
      1234, 2098.65, 124.55, 98.98 ) );
11
12        $oDB->freePrepared( $hQuery );
13        $oDB->disconnect();
14    }
15  ?>
```

Code Listing 29: Using autoPrepare() – UPDATE

If you noticed in Code Listing 28, all three rows that were inserted contained the same *check_number* value. The example in Code Listing 29 updates all rows in the database whose *check_number* is 124. This is accomplished by specifying the *where* parameter in the call to **autoPrepare()**. This is important to note: if you use the DB_AUTOQUERY_UPDATE *mode*, you must specify a value for the *where* parameter otherwise all rows in the table will be affected by the update statement.

⮑ Returns a handle to a prepared query that can be used by the **execute()** and similar methods.

DB_common::autoExecute

❖ *mixed* autoExecute(*string* $table, *array* $fields_values, *int* $mode = DB_AUTOQUERY_INSERT, *mixed* $where = false)

The **autoExecute()** method is a combination of the **autoPrepare()**, **execute()** and **freePrepared()** methods executed in that order.

An example of usage is shown in Code Listing 30. The example illustrates how straightforward updating rows in a database can become when using PEAR::DB to encapsulate a great deal of the work. The code causes the following SQL statement to execute against the database:

```
1    update Paychecks set gross_pay = '3123.45',
     taxes_withheld = '324.43' where ( check_number =
     '1234' )
```

Depending on your application, using the prepare/execute model along with the **autoPrepare()** or **autoExecute()** methods may improve readability and long-term maintenance. If you choose to use some of these methods, it becomes important to note their limitations. With the **autoPrepare()** and **autoExecute()** methods, it is not possible to specify the '!' type of parameter. Therefore the following type of query is impossible to accomplish:

```
1    update Paychecks set taxes_withheld =
     taxes_withheld * 1.10 where ( employee_id = '1' )
```

However, this type of query is not the type that is intended to be used in an **autoPrepare()** or

autoExecute() situation. Think of these methods in places where you are developing web-based forms to collect and update information.

```
1   <?php
2     require_once( 'DB.php' );
3
4     $oDB = DB::connect(
      'mysql://bt_user:bt_pass@207.44.182.3/book_test',
      true );
5     if ( DB::isConnection( $oDB ) )
6     {
7       $aUpdates = array( 'gross_pay' => '3123.45',
8                          'taxes_withheld' => '324.43'
      );
9       $hQuery   = $oDB->autoExecute( 'Paychecks',
      $aUpdates, DB_AUTOQUERY_UPDATE, 'check_number =
      1234' );
10
11      $oDB->disconnect();
12    }
13  ?>
```

Code Listing 30: Using autoExecute()

➲ Returns either DB_OK on success or a DB_Error object on failure.

DB_common::buildManipSQL

❖ *string* buildManipSQL(*string* $table, *array* $table_fields, *int* $mode, *mixed* $where = false)

The **buildManipSQL()** method is used internally by the **autoPrepare()** method to create a parameterized query. The parameters are the same as for the **autoPrepare()** statement except that the *mode* parameter is not optional.

```
1   <?php
2     require_once( 'DB.php' );
3
4     $oDB = DB::connect(
      'mysql://bt_user:bt_pass@207.44.182.3/book_test',
      true );
5     if ( DB::isConnection( $oDB ) )
6     {
7       $sSQL = $oDB->buildManipSQL( 'Paychecks',
      array( 'employee_id', 'check_date', 'check_number',
```

```
       'gross_pay', 'benefits_withheld', 'taxes_withheld'
       ), DB_AUTOQUERY_INSERT );
8          print( "SQL Statement: $sSQL<br><br>" );
9
10      $sSQL = $oDB->buildManipSQL( 'Paychecks',
       array( 'employee_id', 'check_date', 'check_number',
       'gross_pay', 'benefits_withheld', 'taxes_withheld'
       ), DB_AUTOQUERY_UPDATE, 'check_number = 1234' );
11         print( "SQL Statement: $sSQL<br>" );
12
13      $oDB->disconnect();
14    }
15  ?>
```

Code Listing 31: Using buildManipSQL()

The example in Code Listing 31 is used to print the parameterized queries developed in Code Listing 28 and Code Listing 29. The output is shown in Output 12.

```
1   SQL Statement: INSERT INTO Paychecks
    (employee_id,check_date,check_number,gross_pay,bene
    fits_withheld,taxes_withheld) VALUES (?,?,?,?,?,?)
2
3   SQL Statement: UPDATE Paychecks SET employee_id =
    ?,check_date = ?,check_number = ?,gross_pay =
    ?,benefits_withheld = ?,taxes_withheld = ? WHERE
    check_number = 1234
```

Output 12: Examples of using buildManipSQL()

➲ Returns a SQL string formatted for the **prepare()** statement.

DB_common::execute

❖ *mixed* execute(*resource* $stmt, *array* $data)

The **execute()** method is the primary querying method when using the prepare/execute methodology. Several usage examples have been given in the sections regarding the **prepare()** and **autoPrepare()** methods. See Code Listing 25 on page 61, Code Listing 27 on page 63, Code Listing 28 on page 64, Code Listing 29 on page 65.

➲ Returns either a new DB_result object if the underlying result returns a dataset or a DB_Error if there is a database error.

DB_common::executeEmulateQuery

❖ *mixed* executeEmulateQuery(*resource* $stmt, *array* $data)

The **executeEmulateQuery()** method is technically a private method intended to be used internally by the class. Its function is to convert a parameterized query and its related data into a fully-qualified SQL string. This method is used only by database objects whose back-end server does not natively support the prepare/execute methodology.

Since PHP 4 doesn't actually support private methods, the example in Code Listing 32 shows what the results of the **executeEmulateQuery()** are internally. Note, you should not rely on the existence of this method as PHP 5 will support truly private class methods and properties.

```
1   <?php
2     require_once( 'DB.php' );
3
4     $oDB = DB::connect(
      'mysql://bt_user:bt_pass@207.44.182.3/book_test',
      true );
5     if ( DB::isConnection( $oDB ) )
6     {
7       $sSQL = 'insert into Paychecks ( employee_id,
      check_date, check_number, gross_pay,
      benefits_withheld, taxes_withheld ) values ( ?, !,
      ?, ?, ?, ? )';
8
9       $hQuery = $oDB->prepare( $sSQL );
10
11      $sRealSQL = $oDB->executeEmulateQuery( $hQuery,
      array( 1, 'NOW()', 128, 1098.65, 124.55, 98.98 ) );
12      print( "SQL: $sRealSQL<br><br>" );
13
14      $oDB->freePrepared( $hQuery );
15      $oDB->disconnect();
```

```
16    }
17  ?>
```

Code Listing 32: Example of executeEmulateQuery()

The output of Code Listing 32 is shown in Output 13.

```
1   SQL: insert into Paychecks ( employee_id,
    check_date, check_number, gross_pay,
    benefits_withheld, taxes_withheld ) values ( 1,
    NOW(), 128, 1098.65, 124.55, 98.98 )
```

Output 13: Output of executeEmulateQuery() example

⮑ Returns a string containing a fully-qualified query or a DB_Error on failure.

DB_common::executeMultiple

❖ *mixed* executeMultiple(*resource* $stmt, *array* $data)

The **executeMultiple()** method is identical to the **execute()** method except that its *data* parameter is a two-dimensional array. The array can be thought of as data rows.

```
1   <?php
2     require_once( 'DB.php' );
3
4     $oDB = DB::connect(
    'mysql://bt_user:bt_pass@207.44.182.3/book_test',
    true );
5     if ( DB::isConnection( $oDB ) )
6     {
7       $hQuery = $oDB->autoPrepare( 'Paychecks',
    array( 'employee_id', 'check_date', 'check_number',
    'gross_pay', 'benefits_withheld', 'taxes_withheld'
    ) );
8
9       $aAllData[] = array( 1, '2003-11-27', 224,
    1098.65, 124.55, 98.98 );
10      $aAllData[] = array( 2, '2003-11-27', 225,
    1198.65, 124.55, 99.98 );
```

```
11        $aAllData[] = array( 3, '2003-11-27', 226,
     1298.65, 124.55, 95.98 );
12
13        $oDB->executeMultiple( $hQuery, $aAllData );
14        $oDB->freePrepared( $hQuery );
15
16        $oDB->disconnect();
17    }
18  ?>
```

Code Listing 33: Using executeMultiple()

The code in Code Listing 33 illustrates how to use the
executeMultiple() method. This example is
identical to that in Code Listing 28 on page 64 except
that the actual data is passed into the
executeMultiple() as a two-dimensional array.

The internal code for **executeMultiple()** is a simple
array traversal calling **execute()**. If an error occurs
on any given *row* of data, the process aborts and
subsequent rows are not processed.

This is an important consideration for this method
and if there is a chance that a single row may fail, it
may be preferable to use **execute()** in a loop yourself
and handle the error cases as needed.

➲ Returns DB_OK or a DB_Error object.

DB_common::freePrepared

❖ *boolean* freePrepared(*resource* $stmt)

Frees a prepared query handle that was created using
either the **prepare()** or **autoPrepare()** method. For
usage examples, see Code Listing 25, Code Listing 27,
Code Listing 28, Code Listing 29, Code Listing 32 or
Code Listing 33.

➲ Returns true if the passed parameter is a proper query handle, false otherwise.

DB_common::modifyQuery

❖ *string* the modifyQuery(*string* $query)

The **modifyQuery()** method is intended to only be used by the backend database objects. It is a private method that is defined at the DB_common level to ensure that all implementations have at least an empty definition of **modifyQuery()** available.

➲ Returns modified query string from a given input query string.

DB_common::modifyLimitQuery

❖ the modifyLimitQuery(*string* $query, *integer* $from, *integer* $count)

The **modifyLimitQuery()** method is intended to only be used by the backend database objects. It is a private method that is defined at the DB_common level to ensure that all implementations have at least an empty definition of **modifyLimitQuery()** available. See the description of **limitQuery()** on page 74 for usage information.

➲ Returns modified query string from a given input query string.

DB_common::query

❖ *mixed* query(*string* $query, *array* $params = array())

The **query()** method sends a query to the database. If the *params* argument is not specified, then *query* is interpreted as a simple SQL string, otherwise *query* is interpreted to be a parameterized query and is used in conjunction with *params* in a **prepare()** and **execute()** sequence. The example in Code Listing 34 shows both possibilities.

```php
1   <?php
2     require_once( 'DB.php' );
3
4     $oDB = DB::connect(
    'mysql://bt_user:bt_pass@207.44.182.3/book_test',
    true );
5     if ( DB::isConnection( $oDB ) )
6     {
7       $oDB->setFetchMode( DB_FETCHMODE_ASSOC );
8
9       $aSQL  = "select * from Employees where (
    mgr_id = '2' ) or ( mgr_id = '0' )";
10      $oRows = $oDB->query( $aSQL );
11      if ( !DB::isError( $oRows ) )
12      {
13        while ( $aRow = $oRows->fetchRow() )
14        {
15          print( $aRow['first_name'] . ' ' .
    $aRow['last_name'] . '<br>' );
16        }
17      }
18      print( '<br>' );
19
20      $aSQL  = "select * from Employees where (
    mgr_id = ? ) or ( mgr_id = ? )";
21      $oRows = $oDB->query( $aSQL, array( '2', '0' )
    );
22      if ( !DB::isError( $oRows ) )
23      {
24        while ( $aRow = $oRows->fetchRow() )
25        {
26          print( $aRow['first_name'] . ' ' .
    $aRow['last_name'] . '<br>' );
27        }
28      }
29      print( '<br>' );
30
31      $oDB->disconnect();
32    }
33  ?>
```

Code Listing 34: Using query()

The example in Code Listing 34 shows how to use either a simple query (lines 9 – 18) or a parameterized query (lines 20 – 29) in conjunction with the **query()** method. Note that this example is not a good example of using parameterized queries by any means, but a simple example of the **query()** method.

➲ Returns a DB_result object or DB_OK on success, a DB_Error object on failure.

DB_common::limitQuery

❖ *mixed* limitQuery(*string* $query, *integer* $from, *integer* $count, *array* $params = array())

The **limitQuery()** method generates a limited query. The most important note for this method is that it is an experimental method and is not currently supported by all database back ends. The database types fully supporting the **limitQuery()** method are *ibase, mysql, oci8, pgsql* and *sqlite*.

The concept of the **limitQuery()** method is to modify a SQL statement so that its effect is limited to a certain number of data rows. An example (using the MySQL SQL syntax) is shown in Code Listing 35.

```
1  select * from Employees
2  select * from Employees limit 5, 5
```

Code Listing 35: Limiting a MySQL query using SQL.

In line 1 of Code Listing 35, the unlimited query is shown. The result of that query is to return all matching rows (or all rows in this case). The statement in line 2 of Code Listing 35 illustrates the MySQL syntax for limiting the query to return just 5 data rows, starting from the 6th row in the database (index is zero-based for MySQL).

This type of functionality is very useful for paging through large datasets and limiting results to reduce data transmission. However, each back-end database has its own SQL syntax for limiting the number of rows returned, if the concept is supported at all.

The example in Code Listing 36 shows a simple MySQL solution using the **limitQuery()** method. It is the same example as in Code Listing 34, but only showing two rows, starting with the second row. The parameters to the **limitQuery()** method are the same as the **query()** method, but with the additional starting row number and row count (*from* and *count*, respectively).

```php
<?php
  require_once( 'DB.php' );

  $oDB = DB::connect(
'mysql://bt_user:bt_pass@207.44.182.3/book_test',
true );
  if ( DB::isConnection( $oDB ) )
  {
    $oDB->setFetchMode( DB_FETCHMODE_ASSOC );

    $aSQL  = "select * from Employees where (
mgr_id = '2' ) or ( mgr_id = '0' )";
    $oRows = $oDB->limitQuery( $aSQL, 1, 2 );
    if ( !DB::isError( $oRows ) )
    {
      while ( $aRow = $oRows->fetchRow() )
      {
        print( $aRow['first_name'] . ' ' .
$aRow['last_name'] . '<br>' );
      }
    }
    print( '<br>' );

    $aSQL  = "select * from Employees where (
mgr_id = ? ) or ( mgr_id = ? )";
    $oRows = $oDB->limitQuery( $aSQL, 1, 2, array(
'2', '0' ) );
    if ( !DB::isError( $oRows ) )
    {
      while ( $aRow = $oRows->fetchRow() )
      {
        print( $aRow['first_name'] . ' ' .
$aRow['last_name'] . '<br>' );
      }
    }
    print( '<br>' );
```

```
31        $oDB->disconnect();
32    }
33    ?>
```

Code Listing 36: Using limitQuery().

While this type of functionality may be useful to
generalize, I recommend avoiding this method if you
hope to have a database-portable implementation.
Rather, consider the databases that you hope to
support and build a pagination or limiting solution
that will work for your application.

Returns a DB_result object, DB_OK or a DB_Error
object.

DB_common::getOne

❖ *mixed* getOne(*string* $query, *array* $params =
array())

The **getOne()** method is used to return the first
column of the first row of data returned for the SQL
string, *query*. As with the **query()** method, if *params*
are specified, *query* is expected to be a parameterized
query string.

This method is useful in cases where there is a single
value returned by a query such as may be returned
from an aggregate SQL function. The example in
Code Listing 37 shows how to return the total
number of rows in a table using the **getOne()**
method and the equivalent using the **query()** method.

```
1    <?php
2      require_once( 'DB.php' );
3
4      $oDB = DB::connect(
      'mysql://bt_user:bt_pass@207.44.182.3/book_test',
      true );
5        if ( DB::isConnection( $oDB ) )
6        {
```

```
 7        $aSQL  = "select count(*) from Employees";
 8        $oRows = $oDB->query( $aSQL );
 9        if ( !DB::isError( $oRows ) )
10        {
11           while ( $aRow = $oRows->fetchRow() )
12           {
13              print( 'The Employees table has ' .
   $aRow[0] . ' rows.<br>' );
14           }
15        }
16        print( '<br>' );
17
18        $aSQL  = "select count(*) from Employees";
19        $mValue = $oDB->getOne( $aSQL );
20        if ( !DB::isError( $mValue ) )
21        {
22           print( 'The Employees table has ' . $mValue .
   ' rows.<br>' );
23        }
24        print( '<br>' );
25
26        $oDB->disconnect();
27     }
28  ?>
```

Code Listing 37: Using getOne().

Lines 7 – 15 of Code Listing 37 show the typical method to retrieve a single value from a database using **query()**. Lines 18 – 23 show how the **getOne()** method can be used to reduce the coding overhead for simple queries.

An important note for using the **getOne()** method is that the database *fetchmode* **must** be set to DB_FETCHMODE_ORDERED. If you typically use the **setFetchMode()** method to set the database connection object's *fetchmode* to DB_FETCHMODE_ASSOC, you won't get the desired results when using the **getOne()** method.

I feel that I typically gain more coding advantage from using the DB_FETCHMODE_ASSOC setting than by using methods such as **getOne()** to reduce coding effort. Your results may vary.

➲ Returns a DB_Error object, DB_OK or the returned value of the query.

DB_common::getRow

❖ *array* getRow(*string* $query, *array* $params = null,
integer $fetchmode = DB_FETCHMODE_DEFAULT)

This method is similar in concept to the **getOne()** method. The **getRow()** method returns the first row of the result set obtained from the query string, *query*. As with the **query()** method, if *params* is an array, it is assumed that *query* is a parameterized query, and *params* are the actual parameters to use in a prepare/execute query.

The *fetchmode* parameter may be specified when using this method otherwise the value set using **setFetchMode()** will apply to this particular method.

```
1   <?php
2     require_once( 'DB.php' );
3
4     $oDB = DB::connect(
      'mysql://bt_user:bt_pass@207.44.182.3/book_test',
      true );
5     if ( DB::isConnection( $oDB ) )
6     {
7       $aSQL  = "select * from Employees limit 1";
8       $aValue = $oDB->getRow( $aSQL );
9       if ( !DB::isError( $aValue ) )
10      {
11        var_dump( $aValue );
12      }
13
14      $aValue = $oDB->getRow( $aSQL, null,
      DB_FETCHMODE_ASSOC );
15      if ( !DB::isError( $aValue ) )
16      {
17        var_dump( $aValue );
18      }
19
20      $oDB->disconnect();
21    }
22  ?>
```

Code Listing 38: Using getRow().

The sample in Code Listing 38 illustrates general use of the **getOne()** method. Lines 7 – 12 show basic usage. Lines 14 – 18 illustrate the same but use the DB_FETCHMODE_ASSOC value. The output (reformatted for readability) is shown in Output 14.

```
1    array(6) {
2       [0]=>
3       string(1) "1"
4       [1]=>
5       string(11) "Schwendiman"
6       [2]=>
7       string(5) "Blake"
8       [3]=>
9       string(3) "204"
10      [4]=>
11      string(1) "2"
12      [5]=>
13      string(1) "1"
14    }
15    array(6) {
16      ["id"]=>
17      string(1) "1"
18      ["last_name"]=>
19      string(11) "Schwendiman"
20      ["first_name"]=>
21      string(5) "Blake"
22      ["phone_ext"]=>
23      string(3) "204"
24      ["mgr_id"]=>
25      string(1) "2"
26      ["dept_id"]=>
27      string(1) "1"
28    }
```

Output 14: Output of the getRow() method.

➲ Returns a DB_Error object, DB_OK or the returned value of the query.

DB_common::getCol

❖ *array* getCol(*string* $query, *mixed* $col = 0, *array* $params = array())

This method is similar in concept to the **getRow()** method. The **getCol()** method returns the values in the column specified by *col* for all rows of the result

set obtained from the query string, *query*. As with the
query() method, if *params* is an array, it is assumed
that *query* is a parameterized query, and *params* are the
actual parameters to use in a prepare/execute query.

The **getCol()** method does not use a *fetchmode*
parameter and it does not respect the internal
fetchmode set by **setFetchMode()**. If the value of
col is an integer, **getCol()** uses
DB_FETCHMODE_ORDERED internally. If *col* is
a string (column name) then
DB_FETCHMODE_ASSOC is used internally.

```php
1   <?php
2     require_once( 'DB.php' );
3
4     $oDB = DB::connect(
    'mysql://bt_user:bt_pass@207.44.182.3/book_test',
    true );
5     if ( DB::isConnection( $oDB ) )
6     {
7       $aSQL   = "select * from Employees limit 5";
8       $aValue = $oDB->getCol( $aSQL, 'first_name' );
9       if ( !DB::isError( $aValue ) )
10      {
11        var_dump( $aValue );
12      }
13
14      $aValue = $oDB->getCol( $aSQL, 1 );
15      if ( !DB::isError( $aValue ) )
16      {
17        var_dump( $aValue );
18      }
19
20      $oDB->disconnect();
21    }
22  ?>
```

Code Listing 39: Using getCol().

The example in Code Listing 39 shows general use of
the **getCol()** method. Line 10 illustrates making the
call with a string column name, while line 16 shows its
use with an integer column index (column 1 is the
last_name column in this table). The output of the
example code (reformatted for readability) is shown
in Output 15.

```
 1    array(5) {
 2      [0]=>
 3      string(5) "Blake"
 4      [1]=>
 5      string(7) "Jeffrey"
 6      [2]=>
 7      string(4) "Kate"
 8      [3]=>
 9      string(4) "Ryan"
10      [4]=>
11      string(4) "Ryan"
12    }
13    array(5) {
14      [0]=>
15      string(11) "Schwendiman"
16      [1]=>
17      string(3) "Cox"
18      [2]=>
19      string(7) "McNulty"
20      [3]=>
21      string(11) "Schwendiman"
22      [4]=>
23      string(11) "Schwendiman"
24    }
```

Output 15: Output of the getCol() method.

➲ Returns an indexed array with the data from the column specified by the *col* parameter or DB_Error.

DB_common::getAssoc

❖ *array* getAssoc(*string* $query, *boolean* $force_array = false, *array* $params = array(), *integer* $fetchmode = DB_FETCHMODE_DEFAULT, *boolean* $group = false)

The **getAssoc()** method returns the entire result set of a query as an associative array using the first column as the array key. If the result set contains more that two columns, the value of each element in the return array will be an array of values from columns 2 through *n*. If the result set contains only 2 columns, the value of each element in the return array will be a scalar value unless the *force_array* parameter is true. If the result set contains less than two columns, a DB_ERROR_TRUNCATED error is returned.

```
1    <?php
2      require_once( 'DB.php' );
3
4      $oDB = DB::connect(
       'mysql://bt_user:bt_pass@207.44.182.3/book_test',
       true );
5      if ( DB::isConnection( $oDB ) )
6      {
7        $aSQL  = "select * from Employees limit 3";
8        $aValue = $oDB->getAssoc( $aSQL );
9        if ( !DB::isError( $aValue ) )
10       {
11         print( '<pre>' );
12         var_dump( $aValue );
13         print( '</pre>' );
14       }
15
16       $oDB->disconnect();
17     }
18   ?>
```

Code Listing 40: Using getAssoc() – Simplest usage.

The example in Code Listing 40 illustrates the simplest calling convention for the **getAssoc()** method. The output is shown in Output 16.

```
1    array(3) {
2      [1]=>
3      array(5) {
4        [0]=>
5        string(11) "Schwendiman"
6        [1]=>
7        string(5) "Blake"
8        [2]=>
9        string(3) "204"
10       [3]=>
11       string(1) "2"
12       [4]=>
13       string(1) "1"
14     }
15     [2]=>
16     array(5) {
17       [0]=>
18       string(3) "Cox"
19       [1]=>
20       string(7) "Jeffrey"
21       [2]=>
22       string(3) "225"
23       [3]=>
24       string(1) "0"
25       [4]=>
26       string(1) "1"
27     }
28     [3]=>
29     array(5) {
```

```
30        [0]=>
31        string(7) "McNulty"
32        [1]=>
33        string(4) "Kate"
34        [2]=>
35        string(3) "214"
36        [3]=>
37        string(1) "2"
38        [4]=>
39        string(1) "2"
40    }
41  }
```

Output 16: Output of getAssoc() related to Code Listing 40.

Note that the array shown in Output 16 is an associative array where the key is the *id* field of each row of the result set and the values are the other fields of the result set.

The *fetchmode* parameter can be specified to override any global setting made using **setFetchmode()**.

I prefer to use the **setFetchmode()** method, so the example in Code Listing 41 shows this. The output from this change is shown in Output 17.

```
1   <?php
2     require_once( 'DB.php' );
3
4     $oDB = DB::connect(
      'mysql://bt_user:bt_pass@207.44.182.3/book_test',
      true );
5     if ( DB::isConnection( $oDB ) )
6     {
7       $oDB->setFetchMode( DB_FETCHMODE_ASSOC );
8
9       $aSQL   = "select * from Employees limit 3";
10      $aValue = $oDB->getAssoc( $aSQL );
11      if ( !DB::isError( $aValue ) )
12      {
13        print( '<pre>' );
14        var_dump( $aValue );
15        print( '</pre>' );
16      }
17
18      $oDB->disconnect();
19    }
20  ?>
```

Code Listing 41: Using getAssoc() – Example with setFetchmode().

```
1    array(3) {
2      [1]=>
3      array(5) {
4        ["last_name"]=>
5        string(11) "Schwendiman"
6        ["first_name"]=>
7        string(5) "Blake"
8        ["phone_ext"]=>
9        string(3) "204"
10       ["mgr_id"]=>
11       string(1) "2"
12       ["dept_id"]=>
13       string(1) "1"
14     }
15     [2]=>
16     array(5) {
17       ["last_name"]=>
18       string(3) "Cox"
19       ["first_name"]=>
20       string(7) "Jeffrey"
21       ["phone_ext"]=>
22       string(3) "225"
23       ["mgr_id"]=>
24       string(1) "0"
25       ["dept_id"]=>
26       string(1) "1"
27     }
28     [3]=>
29     array(5) {
30       ["last_name"]=>
31       string(7) "McNulty"
32       ["first_name"]=>
33       string(4) "Kate"
34       ["phone_ext"]=>
35       string(3) "214"
36       ["mgr_id"]=>
37       string(1) "2"
38       ["dept_id"]=>
39       string(1) "2"
40     }
41   }
```

Output 17: Output of getAssoc() related to Code Listing 41.

To illustrate the *force_array* parameter, a query returning only two columns is required. The example in Code Listing 42 shows this.

```
1    <?php
2      require_once( 'DB.php' );
3
```

```
4      $oDB = DB::connect(
    'mysql://bt_user:bt_pass@207.44.182.3/book_test',
    true );
5      if ( DB::isConnection( $oDB ) )
6      {
7        $oDB->setFetchMode( DB_FETCHMODE_ASSOC );
8
9        $aSQL    = "select id, last_name from Employees
    limit 3";
10       $aValue = $oDB->getAssoc( $aSQL );
11       if ( !DB::isError( $aValue ) )
12       {
13         print( '<pre>' );
14         var_dump( $aValue );
15         print( '</pre>' );
16       }
17
18       $oDB->disconnect();
19     }
20   ?>
```

**Code Listing 42: Using getAssoc() – Illustrating *force_array*
parameter (set to *false*).**

As can be seen in the output, Output 18, the default
behavior of **getAssoc()** when there are only two
columns in the result set, the resulting array is indexed
by the first column and the second column contains
atomic values.

```
1    array(3) {
2      [1]=>
3      string(11) "Schwendiman"
4      [2]=>
5      string(3) "Cox"
6      [3]=>
7      string(7) "McNulty"
8    }
```

Output 18: Output of getAssoc() related to Code Listing 42.

✒ The advantage of using the *force_array* parameter is
that you can write more generic code to handle the
result array, rather than have special case code for a
result array containing values that are arrays and other
code for a result array containing values that are
atomic.

The example in Code Listing 43 shows the usage of the *force_array* parameter. Its output is shown in Output 19.

```
1   <?php
2     require_once( 'DB.php' );
3
4     $oDB = DB::connect(
      'mysql://bt_user:bt_pass@207.44.182.3/book_test',
      true );
5     if ( DB::isConnection( $oDB ) )
6     {
7        $oDB->setFetchMode( DB_FETCHMODE_ASSOC );
8
9        $aSQL    = "select id, last_name from Employees
      limit 3";
10       $aValue = $oDB->getAssoc( $aSQL, true );
11       if ( !DB::isError( $aValue ) )
12       {
13         print( '<pre>' );
14         var_dump( $aValue );
15         print( '</pre>' );
16       }
17
18       $oDB->disconnect();
19     }
20   ?>
```

Code Listing 43: Using getAssoc() – Illustrating *force_array* parameter (set to *true*).

```
1   array(3) {
2     [1]=>
3     array(1) {
4       ["last_name"]=>
5       string(11) "Schwendiman"
6     }
7     [2]=>
8     array(1) {
9       ["last_name"]=>
10      string(3) "Cox"
11     }
12     [3]=>
13     array(1) {
14       ["last_name"]=>
15       string(7) "McNulty"
16     }
17   }
```

Output 19: Output of getAssoc() related to Code Listing 43.

If the more than one row occurs with the same value in the first column, the last row overwrites all previous ones by default. Use the *group* parameter if you want to retain all results grouped by the value in the first column. To illustrate this, Code Listing 44 contains a query in which the first parameter is a value that repeats in the result set.

```
1   <?php
2     require_once( 'DB.php' );
3
4     $oDB = DB::connect(
   'mysql://bt_user:bt_pass@207.44.182.3/book_test',
   true );
5     if ( DB::isConnection( $oDB ) )
6     {
7        $oDB->setFetchMode( DB_FETCHMODE_ASSOC );
8
9        $aSQL    = "select mgr_id, last_name, first_name
   from Employees";
10       $aValue = $oDB->getAssoc( $aSQL );
11       if ( !DB::isError( $aValue ) )
12       {
13          print( '<pre>' );
14          var_dump( $aValue );
15          print( '</pre>' );
16       }
17
18       $oDB->disconnect();
19    }
20  ?>
```

Code Listing 44: Using getAssoc() – Illustrating *group* parameter (set to *false*).

The output of Code Listing 44 is shown in Output 20. As can be seen, the array consists of only three elements representing the three unique *mgr_id* values in the result set.

```
1   array(3) {
2     [2]=>
3     array(2) {
4        ["last_name"]=>
5        string(7) "McNulty"
6        ["first_name"]=>
7        string(4) "Kate"
8     }
9     [0]=>
10    array(2) {
11       ["last_name"]=>
12       string(3) "Cox"
13       ["first_name"]=>
14       string(7) "Jeffrey"
15    }
```

```
16      [1]=>
17      array(2) {
18        ["last_name"]=>
19        string(11) "Schwendiman"
20        ["first_name"]=>
21        string(6) "Taylor"
22      }
23    }
```

Output 20: Output of getAssoc() related to Code Listing 44.

Since *mgr_id* may be the same for several *Employees*, it is important to set the *group* parameter of the **getAssoc()** method to true to obtain all of the row data. The code in Code Listing 45 illustrates this.

```php
1   <?php
2     require_once( 'DB.php' );
3
4     $oDB = DB::connect(
    'mysql://bt_user:bt_pass@207.44.182.3/book_test',
    true );
5     if ( DB::isConnection( $oDB ) )
6     {
7       $oDB->setFetchMode( DB_FETCHMODE_ASSOC );
8
9       $aSQL    = "select mgr_id, last_name, first_name
    from Employees";
10      $aValue = $oDB->getAssoc( $aSQL, false,
    array(), DB_FETCHMODE_ASSOC, true );
11      if ( !DB::isError( $aValue ) )
12      {
13        print( '<pre>' );
14        var_dump( $aValue );
15        print( '</pre>' );
16      }
17
18      $oDB->disconnect();
19    }
20  ?>
```

Code Listing 45: Using getAssoc() – Illustrating *group* parameter (set to *true*).

Since the *group* parameter is the last parameter of the **getAssoc()** method, all of the intermediate parameters must be specified (see line 10). The output related to this change is shown in Output 21.

```
1   array(3) {
2     [2]=>
```

```
 3    array(2) {
 4      [0]=>
 5      array(2) {
 6        ["last_name"]=>
 7        string(11) "Schwendiman"
 8        ["first_name"]=>
 9        string(5) "Blake"
10      }
11      [1]=>
12      array(2) {
13        ["last_name"]=>
14        string(7) "McNulty"
15        ["first_name"]=>
16        string(4) "Kate"
17      }
18    }
19    [0]=>
20    array(1) {
21      [0]=>
22      array(2) {
23        ["last_name"]=>
24        string(3) "Cox"
25        ["first_name"]=>
26        string(7) "Jeffrey"
27      }
28    }
29    [1]=>
30    array(3) {
31      [0]=>
32      array(2) {
33        ["last_name"]=>
34        string(11) "Schwendiman"
35        ["first_name"]=>
36        string(4) "Ryan"
37      }
38      [1]=>
39      array(2) {
40        ["last_name"]=>
41        string(11) "Schwendiman"
42        ["first_name"]=>
43        string(5) "Scott"
44      }
45      [2]=>
46      array(2) {
47        ["last_name"]=>
48        string(11) "Schwendiman"
49        ["first_name"]=>
50        string(6) "Taylor"
51      }
52    }
53  }
```

Output 21: Output of getAssoc() related to Code Listing 45.

As with the **query()** method, if *params* is an array, it is assumed that *query* is a parameterized query, and *params* are the actual parameters to use in a prepare/execute query.

➲ Returns an associative array containing all of the data from the query string or a DB_Error object.

DB_common::getAll

❖ *array* getAll(*string* $query, *array* $params = null, *integer* $fetchmode = DB_FETCHMODE_DEFAULT)

The **getAll()** method is similar to the **getAssoc()** method, but instead of returning an associative array indexed by the first column of data, **getAll()** returns an indexed array and all of the columns are part of the resulting array values.

The simplest example of using the **getAll()** method is shown in Code Listing 46.

```php
1   <?php
2     require_once( 'DB.php' );
3
4     $oDB = DB::connect(
      'mysql://bt_user:bt_pass@207.44.182.3/book_test',
      true );
5     if ( DB::isConnection( $oDB ) )
6     {
7       $oDB->setFetchmode( DB_FETCHMODE_ASSOC );
8
9       $aSQL   = "select * from Employees";
10      $aValue = $oDB->getAll( $aSQL );
11      if ( !DB::isError( $aValue ) )
12      {
13        print( '<pre>' );
14        var_dump( $aValue );
15        print( '</pre>' );
16      }
17
18      $oDB->disconnect();
19    }
20  ?>
```

Code Listing 46: Using getAll() – Simplest usage.

The output related to Code Listing 46 is shown in Output 22 (output is truncated to first two rows for space).

```
1   array(6) {
2     [0]=>
3     array(6) {
4       ["id"]=>
5       string(1) "1"
6       ["last_name"]=>
7       string(11) "Schwendiman"
8       ["first_name"]=>
9       string(5) "Blake"
10      ["phone_ext"]=>
11      string(3) "204"
12      ["mgr_id"]=>
13      string(1) "2"
14      ["dept_id"]=>
15      string(1) "1"
16    }
17    [1]=>
18    array(6) {
19      ["id"]=>
20      string(1) "2"
21      ["last_name"]=>
22      string(3) "Cox"
23      ["first_name"]=>
24      string(7) "Jeffrey"
25      ["phone_ext"]=>
26      string(3) "225"
27      ["mgr_id"]=>
28      string(1) "0"
29      ["dept_id"]=>
30      string(1) "1"
31    }
```

Output 22: Output of getAll() related to Code Listing 46.

The **getAll()** method is the only method in which the fetchmode can include the DB_FETCHMODE_FLIPPED bit and have any effect. This fetchmode bit indicates that the result array should be first indexed by the columns of the result set and then by the rows of data. As mentioned in the section covering **setFetchMode()** on page 52, the DB_FETCHMODE_FLIPPED bit cannot be set generically using **setFetchmode()** and therefore must be passed specifically into the **getAll()** method. An example of this is shown in Code Listing 47.

```
1   <?php
2     require_once( 'DB.php' );
3
```

```
4      $oDB = DB::connect(
       'mysql://bt_user:bt_pass@207.44.182.3/book_test',
       true );
5      if ( DB::isConnection( $oDB ) )
6      {
7          $aSQL    = "select * from Employees";
8          $aValue = $oDB->getAll( $aSQL, null,
       DB_FETCHMODE_ASSOC + DB_FETCHMODE_FLIPPED );
9          if ( !DB::isError( $aValue ) )
10         {
11             print( '<pre>' );
12             var_dump( $aValue );
13             print( '</pre>' );
14         }
15
16         $oDB->disconnect();
17     }
18 ?>
```

Code Listing 47: Using getAll() – Using DB_FETCHMODE_FLIPPED.

The tiny code change in Code Listing 47 causes the output shown in Output 23. As can be seen in this output, all of the columnar data is grouped together.

```
1   array(6) {
2     ["id"]=>
3     array(6) {
4       [0]=>
5       string(1) "1"
6       [1]=>
7       string(1) "2"
8       [2]=>
9       string(1) "3"
10      [3]=>
11      string(1) "4"
12      [4]=>
13      string(2) "58"
14      [5]=>
15      string(2) "59"
16    }
17    ["last_name"]=>
18    array(6) {
19      [0]=>
20      string(11) "Schwendiman"
21      [1]=>
22      string(3) "Cox"
23      [2]=>
24      string(7) "McNulty"
25      [3]=>
26      string(11) "Schwendiman"
27      [4]=>
28      string(11) "Schwendiman"
29      [5]=>
30      string(11) "Schwendiman"
31    }
32    ["first_name"]=>
```

```
33    array(6) {
34      [0]=>
35      string(5) "Blake"
36      [1]=>
37      string(7) "Jeffrey"
38      [2]=>
39      string(4) "Kate"
40      [3]=>
41      string(4) "Ryan"
42      [4]=>
43      string(5) "Scott"
44      [5]=>
45      string(6) "Taylor"
46    }
```

Output 23: Output of getAll() related to Code Listing 47.

As with the **query()** method, if *params* is an array, it is assumed that *query* is a parameterized query, and *params* are the actual parameters to use in a prepare/execute query.

➲ Returns an associative array containing all of the data from the query string or a DB_Error object.

DB_common::autoCommit

❖ *mixed* autoCommit(*boolean* $onoff = false)

Enables or disables automatic commit for queries. This method is supported only by database engines that support transactions. By default, autocommit is set to true for the transaction-supporting databases.

➲ Returns DB_OK or a DB_Error object on failure.

DB_common::commit

❖ *mixed* commit(*void*)

The **commit()** method commits a transaction against the database. This method is supported only by those DB objects whose backend supports transactions.

```
1   <?php
2     require_once( 'DB.php' );
3
4     $bRollbackCondition = true;
5
6     $oDB = DB::connect(
    'mysql://bt_user:bt_pass@207.44.182.3/book_test',
    true );
7     if ( DB::isConnection( $oDB ) )
8     {
9       $aSQL   = "select * from Employees where (
    mgr_id = 2 )";
10      $aValue = $oDB->getAll( $aSQL );
11      if ( !DB::isError( $aValue ) )
12      {
13        print( '<pre>' );
14        var_dump( $aValue );
15        print( '</pre>' );
16      }
17
18      $oDB->autoCommit( false );
19
20      $aSQL = "update Employees set mgr_id = 3 where
    ( mgr_id = 2 )";
21      $oDB->query( $aSQL );
22      if ( $bRollbackCondition == true )
23      {
24        $result = $oDB->rollback();
25        print( "Updates rolled back<br>" );
26      }
27      else
28      {
29        $result = $oDB->commit();
30        print( "Updates committed<br>" );
31      }
32
33      $aSQL   = "select * from Employees where (
    mgr_id = 2 )";
34      $aValue = $oDB->getAll( $aSQL );
35      if ( !DB::isError( $aValue ) )
36      {
37        print( '<pre>' );
38        var_dump( $aValue );
39        print( '</pre>' );
40      }
41
42      $oDB->disconnect();
43    }
44  ?>
```

Code Listing 48: Using commit().

The very simplistic example shown in Code Listing 48
illustrates how the **commit()** method can be used.
The code uses a simple Boolean value to determine
whether to commit or roll back the transaction, so
this same code can be re-used for the **rollback()**

method example. In practice, other more meaningful factors would be used to determine whether a commit should occur.

Note that for this example to work against a MySQL database, you must have the InnoDB capabilities installed and the *Employees* table must be an INNODB table.

The output generated by the **commit()** example is shown in Output 24. Lines 36 and 37 show that the UPDATE query was successfully committed to the database since the subsequent SELECT query returns an empty result set.

```
1    array(2) {
2      [0]=>
3      array(6) {
4        [0]=>
5        string(1) "1"
6        [1]=>
7        string(11) "Schwendiman"
8        [2]=>
9        string(5) "Blake"
10       [3]=>
11       string(3) "204"
12       [4]=>
13       string(1) "2"
14       [5]=>
15       string(1) "1"
16     }
17     [1]=>
18     array(6) {
19       [0]=>
20       string(1) "3"
21       [1]=>
22       string(7) "McNulty"
23       [2]=>
24       string(4) "Kate"
25       [3]=>
26       string(3) "214"
27       [4]=>
28       string(1) "2"
29       [5]=>
30       string(1) "2"
31     }
32   }
33
34   Updates committed
35
36   array(0) {
37   }
```

Output 24: Example of using commit().

➲ Returns DB_OK or a DB_Error object.

DB_common::rollback

❖ *mixed* rollback(*void*)

The **rollback()** method rolls back a transaction from the database. This method is supported only by those DB objects whose backend supports transactions. See the description of the **commit()** method (page 93) for caveats related to using transactions with MySQL.

```php
<?php
  require_once( 'DB.php' );

  $bRollbackCondition = true;

  $oDB = DB::connect(
  'mysql://bt_user:bt_pass@207.44.182.3/book_test',
  true );
  if ( DB::isConnection( $oDB ) )
  {
    $aSQL    = "select * from Employees where (
  mgr_id = 2 )";
    $aValue = $oDB->getAll( $aSQL );
    if ( !DB::isError( $aValue ) )
    {
      print( '<pre>' );
      var_dump( $aValue );
      print( '</pre>' );
    }

    $oDB->autoCommit( false );

    $aSQL = "update Employees set mgr_id = 3 where
  ( mgr_id = 2 )";
    $oDB->query( $aSQL );
    if ( $bRollbackCondition == true )
    {
      $result = $oDB->rollback();
      print( "Updates rolled back<br>" );
    }
    else
    {
      $result = $oDB->commit();
      print( "Updates committed<br>" );
    }
```

```
33      $aSQL     = "select * from Employees where (
     mgr_id = 2 )";
34      $aValue = $oDB->getAll( $aSQL );
35      if ( !DB::isError( $aValue ) )
36      {
37        print( '<pre>' );
38        var_dump( $aValue );
39        print( '</pre>' );
40      }
41
42      $oDB->disconnect();
43    }
44  ?>
```

Code Listing 49: Using rollback().

The example shown in Code Listing 49 is exactly the same as the code in Code Listing 48 (the **commit()** example) except that the rollback condition flag is set to true. This causes the transaction to roll back. The output shown in Output 25 clearly demonstrates that the UPDATE query was rolled back since the data returned from the SELECT query afterwards contains the same data as prior to the UPDATE query.

```
45  array(2) {
46    [0]=>
47    array(6) {
48      [0]=>
49      string(1) "1"
50      [1]=>
51      string(11) "Schwendiman"
52      [2]=>
53      string(5) "Blake"
54      [3]=>
55      string(3) "204"
56      [4]=>
57      string(1) "2"
58      [5]=>
59      string(1) "1"
60    }
61    [1]=>
62    array(6) {
63      [0]=>
64      string(1) "3"
65      [1]=>
66      string(7) "McNulty"
67      [2]=>
68      string(4) "Kate"
69      [3]=>
70      string(3) "214"
71      [4]=>
72      string(1) "2"
73      [5]=>
```

```
74        string(1) "2"
75    }
76  }
77
78  Updates rolled back
79
80  array(2) {
81    [0]=>
82    array(6) {
83      [0]=>
84      string(1) "1"
85      [1]=>
86      string(11) "Schwendiman"
87      [2]=>
88      string(5) "Blake"
89      [3]=>
90      string(3) "204"
91      [4]=>
92      string(1) "2"
93      [5]=>
94      string(1) "1"
95    }
96    [1]=>
97    array(6) {
98      [0]=>
99      string(1) "3"
100     [1]=>
101     string(7) "McNulty"
102     [2]=>
103     string(4) "Kate"
104     [3]=>
105     string(3) "214"
106     [4]=>
107     string(1) "2"
108     [5]=>
109     string(1) "2"
110   }
111 }
```

Output 25: Example of using rollback().

➲ Returns DB_OK or a DB_Error object.

DB_common::numRows

❖ *mixed* numRows(*mixed* $result)

The **numRows()** method may be used to return the number of rows in a DB_result object. I do not recommend using this method (see below), but an example of usage is provided in Code Listing 50.

```
1   <?php
```

```
2    require_once( 'DB.php' );
3
4    $oDB = DB::connect(
     'mysql://bt_user:bt_pass@207.44.182.3/book_test',
     true );
5    if ( DB::isConnection( $oDB ) )
6    {
7      $aSQL  = "select * from Employees";
8      $oRows = $oDB->query( $aSQL );
9      if ( !DB::isError( $oRows ) )
10     {
11        print( 'Number of rows = ' . $oDB->numRows(
       $oRows->result ) . '<br>' );
12     }
13
14     $oDB->disconnect();
15   }
16 ?>
```

Code Listing 50: Using numRows().

Because the parameter, *result*, is required to be a database-specific result identifier, I recommend using the **DB_result::numRows()** method instead (see page 115). By using the latter method, better OO programming practices are employed.

➲ Returns an integer number of rows or a DB_Error object.

DB_common::affectedRows

❖ *mixed* affectedRows(*void*)

The **affectedRows()** method returns the number of rows affected by a database manipulation query such as an INSERT, UPDATE or DELETE query. The example in Code Listing 51 shows its use.

```
17 <?php
18   require_once( 'DB.php' );
19
20   $oDB = DB::connect(
     'mysql://bt_user:bt_pass@207.44.182.3/book_test',
     true );
21   if ( DB::isConnection( $oDB ) )
```

```
22   {
23      $aSQL   = "delete from Paychecks";
24      $oRows  = $oDB->query( $aSQL );
25      if ( !DB::isError( $aValue ) )
26      {
27         print( 'Number of rows deleted = ' . $oDB-
    >affectedRows() . '<br>' );
28      }
29
30      $oDB->disconnect();
31   }
32 ?>
```

Code Listing 51: Using affectedRows().

➲ Returns an integer number of rows or a DB_Error object.

DB_common::errorNative

❖ *mixed* errorNative(*void*)

For details about and examples of **errorNative()** and its relationship with **errorCode()**, see the documentation for **errorCode()** on page 46.

➲ Returns a native error message or code based on the back-end database.

DB_common::nextId

❖ *mixed* nextId(*string* $seq_name, *boolean* $ondemand = true)

The **nextId()** method returns the next available id for the given sequence, *seq_name*. If *ondemand* is true, the sequence is created if it does not already exist. See the section on sequences, starting on page 22 for complete details of sequences and examples of the **nextId()** method.

➲ Returns an integer identifier or a DB_Error object.

DB_common::createSequence

❖ *mixed* createSequence(*string* $seq_name)

The **createSequence()** method creates a new sequence for the database called *seq_name*. See the section on sequences, starting on page 22 for complete details of sequences and examples of using sequences. The **createSequence()** method may be called automatically by the **nextId()** method (see **nextId()** on page 100).

Based on the DB backend used, you may need certain access permissions to successfully use the **createSequence()** method. As an example, the code in Code Listing 52 shows how a user with restricted access cannot create a sequence. The user in the example has only the SELECT privilege on the MySQL database.

```php
<?php
  require_once( 'DB.php' );

  $oDB = DB::connect(
'mysql://bt_r_user:bt_r_pass@207.44.182.3/book_test
', true );
  if ( DB::isConnection( $oDB ) )
  {
    $result = $oDB->createSequence( 'NewSequence'
);
    if ( !DB::isError( $result ) )
    {
      print( 'Sequence created<br>' );
    }
    else
    {
      print( $result->userinfo );
    }

    $oDB->disconnect();
  }
  else
  {
    print( $oDB->userinfo );
  }
?>
```

Code Listing 52: Using createSequence() with MySQL.

Because the user *bt_r_user* does not have permission to create a new table on the *book_test* database, the call to **createSequence()** fails with the output shown in Output 26. Other database servers may have different requirements as to the creation of sequences that may affect the use of the **createSequence()** method. These differences should be considered in any application that uses PEAR::DB sequences.

```
1    CREATE TABLE NewSequence_seq (id INTEGER UNSIGNED
     AUTO_INCREMENT NOT NULL, PRIMARY KEY(id))
     [nativecode=1142 ** create command denied to user:
     'bt_r_user@xxx.xxx.xxx.xxx' for table
     'NewSequence_seq']
```

Output 26: Output of createSequence() on MySQL database with insufficient user privileges.

➲ Returns DB_OK or a DB_Error object.

DB_common::dropSequence

❖ *mixed* dropSequence(*string* $seq_name)

The **dropSequence()** method is the corollary to the **createSequence()** method. The same restrictions regarding security and user privileges apply. See the **createSequence()** method description for details (page 101).

➲ Returns DB_OK or a DB_Error object.

DB_common::tableInfo

❖ *mixed* tableInfo(*mixed* $result, *mixed* $mode = null)

The **tableInfo()** method is used to return metadata information about a table or query. The *result* parameter is a database-specific value available through a DB_result object. As with the **numRows()** method (page 98), the preferred coding method for using **tableInfo()** is through the **DB_result::tableInfo()** method. It is just better OO programming.

In fact, because it is so much better practice, I will not fully document this method here, but refer you to the **DB_result::tableInfo()** method on page 116 for details.

There is one case in which **DB_common::tableInfo()** should be used and that is when you need to obtain metadata about a table that is not associated with a DB_result. In this case, the *result* parameter is a string – the table name.

```php
1    <?php
2      require_once( 'DB.php' );
3
4      $oDB = DB::connect(
       'mysql://bt_user:bt_pass@207.44.182.3/book_test',
       true );
5      if ( DB::isConnection( $oDB ) )
6      {
7        $result = $oDB->tableInfo( 'Employees' );
8        if ( !DB::isError( $result ) )
9        {
10         print( '<pre>' );
11         var_dump( $result );
12         print( '</pre>' );
13       }
14
15       $oDB->disconnect();
16     }
17   ?>
```

Code Listing 53: Using tableInfo().

The example in Code Listing 53 illustrates how to use **tableInfo()** to obtain information about a MySQL database table. The results of a call to **tableInfo()** are database specific. More information about the results is given later in the database-specific sections and in the description of the **DB_result::tableInfo()** method on page 116. Truncated output is shown in Output 27.

```
1   array(6) {
2     [0]=>
3     array(5) {
4       ["table"]=>
5       string(9) "Employees"
6       ["name"]=>
7       string(2) "id"
8       ["type"]=>
9       string(3) "int"
10      ["len"]=>
11      int(11)
12      ["flags"]=>
13      string(20) "not_null primary_key"
14    }
15    [1]=>
16    array(5) {
17      ["table"]=>
18      string(9) "Employees"
19      ["name"]=>
20      string(9) "last_name"
21      ["type"]=>
22      string(6) "string"
23      ["len"]=>
24      int(50)
25      ["flags"]=>
26      string(8) "not_null"
27    }
28    [2]=>
29    array(5) {
30      ["table"]=>
31      string(9) "Employees"
32      ["name"]=>
33      string(10) "first_name"
34      ["type"]=>
35      string(6) "string"
36      ["len"]=>
37      int(50)
38      ["flags"]=>
39      string(8) "not_null"
40    }
```

Output 27: Output of the tableInfo() method.

➲ Returns a DB_Error object or an array containing metadata describing the table or query result.

DB_common::getTables

❖ *mixed* getTables(*void*)

The **getTables()** method returns an array containing all of the tables in the current database.

```php
<?php
  require_once( 'DB.php' );

  $oDB = DB::connect(
  'mysql://bt_user:bt_pass@207.44.182.3/book_test',
  true );
  if ( DB::isConnection( $oDB ) )
  {
    $result = $oDB->getTables();
    if ( !DB::isError( $result ) )
    {
      print( '<pre>' );
      var_dump( $result );
      print( '</pre>' );
    }

    $oDB->disconnect();
  }
?>
```

Code Listing 54: Using getTables().

The output of the example shown in Code Listing 54 is given in Output 28.

```
array(9) {
  [0]=>
  string(11) "Departments"
  [1]=>
  string(9) "Employees"
  [2]=>
  string(9) "Paychecks"
  [3]=>
  string(13) "UploadedFiles"
  [4]=>
  string(13) "seq_employees"
  [5]=>
  string(14) "seq_sequence_1"
  [6]=>
  string(14) "seq_sequence_2"
  [7]=>
  string(14) "sequence_1_seq"
  [8]=>
  string(14) "sequence_2_seq"
}
```

Comprehensive PHP PEAR::DB

Output 28: Output related to getTables example (Code Listing 54).

➲ Returns an indexed array containing the tables in the current database or DB_Error.

DB_common::getListOf

❖ *mixed* getListOf(*string* $type)

The **getListOf()** method returns database-specific information and metadata based on the *type* parameter. The **getTables()** method described on page 105, for example, is a call to **getListOf()** where the *type* parameter is set to the string, 'tables'. The value of the *type* parameter is database specific. Currently the matrix shown in Table 7 lists the support of the *type* parameter by the available databases.

	tables	views	master	schema	functions	users	databases
dbase	□	□	□	□	□	□	□
fbsql	■	□	□	□	□	□	□
ibase	■	□	□	□	□	□	□
ifx	■	□	□	□	□	□	□
msql	■	□	□	□	□	□	□
mssql	■	■	□	□	□	□	□
mysql	■	□	□	□	□	■	■
oci8	■	□	□	□	□	□	□

odbc	☐	☐	☐	☐	☐	☐	☐
pgsql	■	■	☐	☐	■	■	■
sqlite	■	☐	■	■	☐	☐	☐
sybase	■	■	☐	☐	☐	☐	☐
dbase	☐	☐	☐	☐	☐	☐	☐

Table 7: Types supported in getSpecialQuery for each database back end.

```php
<?php
  require_once( 'DB.php' );

  $oDB = DB::connect(
'mysql://bt_user:bt_pass@207.44.182.3/book_test',
true );
  if ( DB::isConnection( $oDB ) )
  {
    print( 'Tables:<ol>' );
    $result = $oDB->getListOf( 'tables' );
    if ( !DB::isError( $result ) )
    {
      foreach ( $result as $aValue )
        print( "<li>$aValue</li>" );
    }
    print( '</ol>' );

    print( 'Users:<ol>' );
    $result = $oDB->getListOf( 'users' );
    if ( !DB::isError( $result ) )
    {
      foreach ( $result as $aValue )
        print( "<li>$aValue</li>" );
    }
    print( '</ol>' );

    print( 'Databases:<ol>' );
    $result = $oDB->getListOf( 'databases' );
    if ( !DB::isError( $result ) )
    {
      foreach ( $result as $aValue )
        print( "<li>$aValue</li>" );
    }
    print( '</ol>' );

    $oDB->disconnect();
  }
?>
```

Code Listing 55: Using getListOf().

The example in Code Listing 55 illustrates the usage of **getListOf()**. As can be seen from the output in Output 29, not only are the types of lists database dependant, but the information available is strictly dependent on user access privileges. There are many more databases on the MySQL server used for this book, but only one is listed because it is the only one available to the specified user. Also, the user name used in the examples here does not have privileges to look into the MySQL user database to list the other users.

```
1    Tables:
2
3    1. Departments
4    2. Employees
5    3. Paychecks
6    4. UploadedFiles
7    5. seq_employees
8    6. seq_sequence_1
9    7. seq_sequence_2
10   8. sequence_1_seq
11   9. sequence_2_seq
12
13   Users:
14
15   Databases:
16
17   1. book_test
```

Output 29: Output of the getListOf() example (Code Listing 55).

➲ Returns a DB_result or DB_Error object.

DB_common::getSequenceName

❖ *string* getSequenceName(*string* $sqn)

This is a private method used by the sequence functions (see page 22). This method returns a fully-qualified sequence name from a simple sequence identifier string, *sqn.*

➲ Returns a string.

Class DB_result

The class DB_result provides methods for working with the results generated by queries on a database. DB_result objects are not likely to be created by your applications directly.

Method	Description
setOption()	Sets options on the DB_result object.
fetchRow()	Fetch and return a row of data. Uses fetchInto internally.
fetchInto()	Fetch a row of data into an existing variable.
numCols()	Returns the number of columns in a result set.
numRows()	Returns the number of rows in a result set.
nextResult()	Returns the next result if a batch of queries was executed.
free()	Free the resources allocated for this result set.
tableInfo()	Returns metadata about the result set.
getRowCounter()	Returns the actual row number.

Table 8: DB_result Class Methods

DB_result::setOption

❖ *void* setOption(*string* $key, *mixed* $value = null)

The **setOption()** method sets the option specified by *key* to the value specified by *value*. There are two options that can be set, 'limit_from' and 'limit_count', both of which are integer values. These options are used internally by the fetch functions and may be dependant on the back end database. In my tests with the *odbc* and *mysql* databases, I found that the 'limit_from' option only works correctly with *odbc*.

🖋 As the usefulness of these options is questionable, I recommend thorough testing of any application that makes use of these options and recommend that you avoid these options if the goal of your application is database portability.

➲ Returns nothing.

DB_result::fetchRow

❖ *mixed* fetchRow(*int* $fetchmode = DB_FETCHMODE_DEFAULT, *int* $rownum = NULL)

The **fetchRow()** method is the primary method used to actually retrieve a row of data into a result variable. Internally the **fetchRow()** method calls **fetchInto()** to perform the actual database-level data retrieval.

The *fetchmode* parameter is one of the pre-defined values: DB_FETCHMODE_ORDERED, DB_FETCHMODE_ASSOC or DB_FETCHMODE_OBJECT. Details about the *fetchmode* parameter can be found in the documentation of **DB_common::setFetchmode()**

on page 52. The *rownum* parameter specifies the row of data to retrieve.

Examples of usage related to the *setfetchmode* parameter can be found in Code Listing 21 on page 53, Code Listing 22 on page 55 and Code Listing 23 on page 56.

The example in Code Listing 56 shows the effects of using the *rownum* parameter.

```php
<?php
  error_reporting( E_ALL );
  require_once( 'DB.php' );

  $oDB = DB::connect(
'mysql://bt_user:bt_pass@207.44.182.3/book_test',
true );
  if ( DB::isConnection( $oDB ) )
  {
    $oDB->setFetchMode( DB_FETCHMODE_ASSOC );

    $sSQL = "select first_name, last_name from
Employees";
    $oRows = $oDB->query( $sSQL );
    if ( !DB::isError( $oRows ) )
    {
      while ( $aRow = $oRows->fetchRow() )
      {
        print( $aRow['first_name'] . ' ' .
$aRow['last_name'] . '<br>' );
      }
      print( '<br>By rownum:<br><br>' );
      // now try to print rows 1, 3, 5 and 7
      $aRow = $oRows->fetchRow( DB_FETCHMODE_ASSOC,
1 );
      print( $aRow['first_name'] . ' ' .
$aRow['last_name'] . '<br>' );
      $aRow = $oRows->fetchRow( DB_FETCHMODE_ASSOC,
3 );
      print( $aRow['first_name'] . ' ' .
$aRow['last_name'] . '<br>' );
      $aRow = $oRows->fetchRow( DB_FETCHMODE_ASSOC,
5 );
      print( $aRow['first_name'] . ' ' .
$aRow['last_name'] . '<br>' );
      $aRow = $oRows->fetchRow( DB_FETCHMODE_ASSOC,
7 );
      print( $aRow['first_name'] . ' ' .
$aRow['last_name'] . '<br>' );

      $oRows->free();
    }
    $oDB->disconnect();
  }
```

```
33    ?>
```

Code Listing 56: Using fetchRow() with a specified
rownum.

As can be seen from the output in Output 30, the
rownum parameter is a zero-based value. When the
rownum is outside of the bounds of the data (as in line
26) no value is returned and no errors or warnings are
generated.

```
1    Blake Schwendiman
2    Jeffrey Cox
3    Kate McNulty
4    Ryan Schwendiman
5    Scott Schwendiman
6    Taylor Schwendiman
7
8    By rownum:
9
10   Jeffrey Cox
11   Ryan Schwendiman
12   Taylor Schwendiman
```

Output 30: Results of fetchRow() from Code Listing 56.

✐ While the availability of *rownum* may provide some
coding simplicity in a few cases, I strongly
recommend against using this feature. The first
reason is that the concept of a row number is not
supported by all PEAR::DB databases, so there is a
database portability problem. The second is that
there are very few times when seeking to a row within
a result set is even necessary. Typically a good SQL
statement initially will create a result set that can be
traversed directly without requiring any seeks.

➲ Returns an array of data, a data object or NULL if
there is no more data.

DB_result::fetchInto

❖ *mixed* fetchInto(*mixed* $arr, *integer* $fetchmode = DB_FETCHMODE_DEFAULT, *integer* $rownum = null)

The **fetchInto()** method is the internal method used by **fetchRow()**. While **fetchInto()** is listed as a public method, I cannot find any compelling reason to suggest its use over the **fetchRow()** method.

```php
<?php
  error_reporting( E_ALL );
  require_once( 'DB.php' );

  $oDB = DB::connect(
'mysql://bt_user:bt_pass@207.44.182.3/book_test',
true );
  if ( DB::isConnection( $oDB ) )
  {
    $oDB->setFetchMode( DB_FETCHMODE_ASSOC );

    $sSQL = "select first_name, last_name from
Employees";
    $oRows = $oDB->query( $sSQL );
    if ( !DB::isError( $oRows ) )
    {
      while ( $oRows->fetchInto( $aRow ) )
      {
        print( $aRow['first_name'] . ' ' .
$aRow['last_name'] . '<br>' );
      }
      print( '<br>By rownum:<br><br>' );
      // now try to print rows 1, 3, 5 and 7
      $oRows->fetchInto( $aRow, DB_FETCHMODE_ASSOC,
1 );
        print( $aRow['first_name'] . ' ' .
$aRow['last_name'] . '<br>' );
      $oRows->fetchInto( $aRow, DB_FETCHMODE_ASSOC,
3 );
        print( $aRow['first_name'] . ' ' .
$aRow['last_name'] . '<br>' );
      $oRows->fetchInto( $aRow, DB_FETCHMODE_ASSOC,
5 );
        print( $aRow['first_name'] . ' ' .
$aRow['last_name'] . '<br>' );
      $oRows->fetchInto( $aRow, DB_FETCHMODE_ASSOC,
7 );
        print( $aRow['first_name'] . ' ' .
$aRow['last_name'] . '<br>' );

      $oRows->free();
    }
    $oDB->disconnect();
  }
?>
```

Code Listing 57: Using fetchInto().

The example in Code Listing 57 is the same as Code Listing 56 but uses **fetchInto()** rather than **fetchRow()**. The output is shown in Output 31. The one notable difference in the output is that the last line seems to indicate that there is data in the row indexed by *rownum* 7. However the output is generated because the argument passed in line 26 of the code (*aRow*) is already set to a value because of its use on line 24.

This is an important difference between **fetchRow()** and **fetchInto()** that you must consider if you choose to use the **fetchInto()** method. Always clear the variable you pass as the first parameter to **fetchInto()** or you may end up with residual data.

```
1   Blake Schwendiman
2   Jeffrey Cox
3   Kate McNulty
4   Ryan Schwendiman
5   Scott Schwendiman
6   Taylor Schwendiman
7
8   By rownum:
9
10  Jeffrey Cox
11  Ryan Schwendiman
12  Taylor Schwendiman
13  Taylor Schwendiman
```

Output 31: Results of fetchInto example (Code Listing 57).

➲ Returns null or DB_OK.

DB_result::numCols

❖ *mixed* numCols(*void*)

Use the **numCols()** method to return the number of columns in the result set. A usage example is given in Code Listing 58 on page 117.

⮑ Returns the number of columns, or a DB_Error object.

DB_result::numRows

❖ *mixed* numRows(*void*)

Use the **numRows()** method to determine the number of rows in the result set.

⮑ Returns the number of rows, or a DB_Error object.

DB_result::nextResult

❖ *bool* nextResult(*void*)

The **nextResult()** method moves the internal result pointer to the next full result set. This method is not implemented for all database back ends. The database types that do support multiple result sets and the **nextResult()** method are *fbsql*, *mssql*, and *odbc*.

☞ Since this method is generally unavailable, it is recommended that you do not use this method if your programming goal is database portability.

⮑ Returns true if another result is available; false if not.

DB_result::free

❖ *mixed* free(*void*)

Frees the resources allocate to the result object.

⮑ Returns true on success, DB_Error object on failure.

DB_result::tableInfo

❖ *mixed* tableInfo(*mixed* $mode = null)

The **tableInfo()** method returns database structure metadata about the result object. One usage example was given in the discussion of **DB_common::tableInfo()** on page 102.

The example shown in Code Listing 58 is a more general purpose example showing the way that the **tableInfo()** metadata can be used in real applications.

```php
1   <?php
2     error_reporting( E_ALL );
3     require_once( 'DB.php' );
4
5     function dbResultToTable( $oDBResult )
6     {
7       $numCols = $oDBResult->numCols();
8
9       $aMetaData = $oDBResult->tableInfo();
10      print( '<table border="1">' );
11
12      // print header row
13      print( '<tr>' );
14      for ( $iIndex = 0; $iIndex < $numCols;
    $iIndex++ )
15      {
16        print( '<td>' . $aMetaData[$iIndex]['name'] .
    '</td>' );
17      }
18      print( '</tr>' );
19
20      // now print all data rows
21      while ( $oData = $oDBResult->fetchRow() )
22      {
23        print( '<tr>' );
24        for ( $iIndex = 0; $iIndex < $numCols;
    $iIndex++ )
25        {
26          print( '<td>' . $oData[$iIndex] . '</td>'
    );
27        }
28        print( '</tr>' );
29      }
30
31      print( '</table>' );
32    }
33
34    $oDB = DB::connect(
    'mysql://bt_user:bt_pass@207.44.182.3/book_test',
    true );
35    if ( DB::isConnection( $oDB ) )
36    {
```

```
37      $oResult = $oDB->query( 'select * from
    Employees' );
38      if ( !DB::isError( $oResult ) )
39      {
40        dbResultToTable( $oResult );
41      }
42
43      $oDB->disconnect();
44    }
45  ?>
```

Code Listing 58: Using tableInfo().

The example code uses **tableInfo()** and **numCols()** to take any generic DB_result and convert it into an HTML table. The image in Figure 5 shows the output of this example.

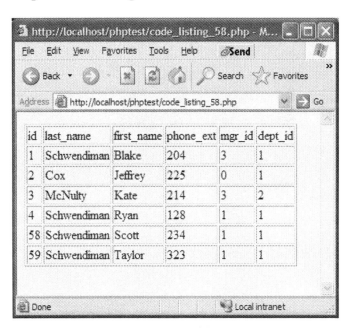

Figure 5: Browser-based output of Code Listing 58.

The *mode* parameter can be one of DB_TABLEINFO_ORDER, DB_TABLEINFO_ORDERTABLE or DB_TABLEINFO_FULL. The last value,

DB_TABLEINFO_FULL, is the combination of the previous values. The *mode* parameter indicates that the method should provide other relevant data in the result array.

```php
<?php
   error_reporting( E_ALL );
   require_once( 'DB.php' );

   $oDB = DB::connect(
'mysql://bt_user:bt_pass@207.44.182.3/book_test',
true );
   if ( DB::isConnection( $oDB ) )
   {
      $oResult = $oDB->query( 'select
Employees.last_name, Departments.name from
Employees, Departments where ( Employees.dept_id =
Departments.id )' );
      if ( !DB::isError( $oResult ) )
      {
         print( 'tableInfo: <br>' );
         $aMetaData = $oResult->tableInfo();
         print( '<pre>' );
         var_dump( $aMetaData );
         print( '</pre>' );

         print( 'tableInfo - DB_TABLEINFO_ORDER: <br>'
);
         $aMetaData = $oResult-
>tableInfo(DB_TABLEINFO_ORDER);
         print( '<pre>' );
         var_dump( $aMetaData );
         print( '</pre>' );

         print( 'tableInfo - DB_TABLEINFO_ORDERTABLE:
<br>' );
         $aMetaData = $oResult-
>tableInfo(DB_TABLEINFO_ORDERTABLE);
         print( '<pre>' );
         var_dump( $aMetaData );
         print( '</pre>' );

         print( 'tableInfo - DB_TABLEINFO_FULL: <br>'
);
         $aMetaData = $oResult-
>tableInfo(DB_TABLEINFO_FULL);
         print( '<pre>' );
         var_dump( $aMetaData );
         print( '</pre>' );
      }

      $oDB->disconnect();
   }
?>
```

Code Listing 59: The *mode* parameter of the tableInfo() method.

The example in Code Listing 59 shows the various *mode* values that can be used with the **tableInfo()** method. The output in Output 32 shows the output of this example. Some of the output text has been omitted to reduce its size.

```
1   tableInfo:
2
3   array(2) {
4     [0]=>
5     array(5) {
6       ["table"]=>
7       string(9) "Employees"
8       ["name"]=>
9       string(9) "last_name"
10      ["type"]=>
11      string(6) "string"
12      ["len"]=>
13      int(50)
14      ["flags"]=>
15      string(8) "not_null"
16    }
17    [1]=>
18    array(5) {
19      ["table"]=>
20      string(11) "Departments"
21      ["name"]=>
22      string(4) "name"
23      ["type"]=>
24      string(6) "string"
25      ["len"]=>
26      int(50)
27      ["flags"]=>
28      string(8) "not_null"
29    }
30  }
31
32  tableInfo - DB_TABLEINFO_ORDER:
33
34  array(4) {
35    ["num_fields"]=>
36    int(2)
37    ["order"]=>
38    array(2) {
39      ["last_name"]=>
40      int(0)
41      ["name"]=>
42      int(1)
43    }
44    * also contains all of lines 4 - 29 above *
45  }
46
47  tableInfo - DB_TABLEINFO_ORDERTABLE:
48
49  array(4) {
```

```
50    ["num_fields"]=>
51    int(2)
52    ["ordertable"]=>
53    array(2) {
54      ["Employees"]=>
55      array(1) {
56        ["last_name"]=>
57        int(0)
58      }
59      ["Departments"]=>
60      array(1) {
61        ["name"]=>
62        int(1)
63      }
64    }
65    * also contains all of lines 4 - 29 above *
66  }
67
68  tableInfo - DB_TABLEINFO_FULL:
69
70  array(5) {
71    ["num_fields"]=>
72    int(2)
73    ["order"]=>
74    array(2) {
75      ["last_name"]=>
76      int(0)
77      ["name"]=>
78      int(1)
79    }
80    ["ordertable"]=>
81    array(2) {
82      ["Employees"]=>
83      array(1) {
84        ["last_name"]=>
85        int(0)
86      }
87      ["Departments"]=>
88      array(1) {
89        ["name"]=>
90        int(1)
91      }
92    }
93    * also contains all of lines 4 - 29 above *
94  }
```

Output 32: The *mode* parameter of the tableInfo() method.

The **tableInfo()** method is only supported by the *fbsql, ibase, mssql, oci8,* and *pgsql* databases. Again, you should not rely on this method if your development goal is database portability.

➲ Returns a database-specific result array or a DB_Error object.

DB_result::getRowCounter

❖ *mixed* getRowCounter(*void*)

The **getRowCounter()** method is intended to retrieve the current row number from the result set. This method relies on the 'limit_from' and 'limit_count' options described in the **setOptions()** method on page 110.

🎗 Because of the caveats mentioned in that section, I recommend against relying on the **getRowCounter()** method as well.

Simulating a row counter in an application is trivial, so I recommending an application-specific row numbering system based on the needs of your specific application.

➲ Returns an integer row number or NULL.

Class DB_Error

The class DB_Error is a subclass of PEAR_Error which is a generic error object used throughout the PEAR classes. A complete description of the PEAR_Error class is out of the scope of this document, but a good example of using DB_Error is illustrated in Code Listing 20 on page 52.

Class DB_Warning

Class DB_Warning has been deprecated and is no longer used in PEAR::DB.

Class DB_storage

The DB_storage class appears to be completely undocumented elsewhere, but as it still ships as part of the PEAR::DB installation, I will cover it here. The concept of DB_storage is to provide a completely object oriented interface into a row of data in a database.

The code in Code Listing 60 shows the basic usage of DB_storage and its relationship with the other PEAR::DB classes already covered in this book.

```php
<?php
    error_reporting( E_ALL );
    require_once( 'DB.php' );
    require_once( 'DB/storage.php' );

    $oDB = DB::connect(
'mysql://bt_user:bt_pass@207.44.182.3/book_test',
true );
    if ( DB::isConnection( $oDB ) )
    {
        // create a new DB_storage object against the
Employees table
        $oStorage = new DB_storage( 'Employees', 'id',
$oDB );

        // initialize this object with the Employee
whose id = 1
        $oStorage->setup( 1 );

        // dump this object to the browser
        print( 'initial data<br>' );
        $oStorage->dump();

        // change the phone extension of this object
        $oStorage->set( 'phone_ext', 2204 );

        // save the changes to the database
        $oStorage->store();

        // dump this object to the browser
        print( '<br>current data<br>' );
        $oStorage->dump();

        $oDB->disconnect();
    }
    else
    {
        var_dump( $oDB );
```

```
34    }
35    ?>
```

Code Listing 60: Overview of the DB_storage Class.

The output from Code Listing 60 is shown in Figure 6. As is clear from the example, the DB_storage class simply provides a basic OO wrapper for a single row in a database.

There is an optional forth argument to the DB_storage constructor that specifies a data validation callback. An example of its use is shown in Code Listing 64 on page 132.

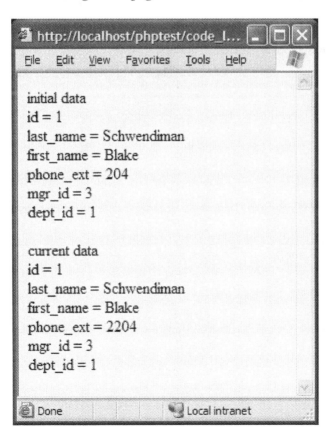

Figure 6: Output of DB_storage overview code.

The DB_storage class provides the framework for developing extremely object-oriented database applications. While I personally advocate OO programming, I am not convinced that using DB_storage in PHP applications gains much when compared to using the array-based data provided by default from the PEAR::DB fetch methods. In large applications with long lifetimes, an OO approach to low-level data manipulation is probably preferred, but many (if not most) PHP applications are short lived and stateless, so this approach may be overkill.

In any case, the methods of the DB_storage class a listed in Table 9 and detailed below.

Method	Description
_makeWhere()	Private method used to generate a WHERE clause to locate the record in the table representing this object.
setup()	Initialize the DB_storage object from the configured table.
insert()	Create a new, empty row in the table for this object.
toString()	Output a simple description of this DB_storage object.
dump()	Dump the contents of this object to *standard output*.
create()	Static method used to create new DB_storage objects.
set()	Modify an attribute of this object.
get()	Fetch an attribute of this object.
store()	Saves changes to this object to the database.

Comprehensive PHP PEAR::DB

| remove() | Remove the row of data associated with this object from the database. |

Table 9: DB_storage Class Methods

DB_storage::_makeWhere

❖ *string* _makeWhere(*mixed* $keyval = null)

This is a private method. If you are using DB_storage, don't use this method.

➲ Returns a string.

DB_storage::setup

❖ *mixed* setup(*mixed* $keyval)

The **setup()** method is used to configure the current object based on the data in the row represented by the key(s) in *keyval*. The value of *keyval* is either an atomic value if the primary key of the table is a single column or an array of values if the primary key is multi-columnar.

```php
<?php
  error_reporting( E_ALL );
  require_once( 'DB.php' );
  require_once( 'DB/storage.php' );

  $oDB = DB::connect(
'mysql://bt_user:bt_pass@207.44.182.3/book_test',
true );
  if ( DB::isConnection( $oDB ) )
  {
    // create a new DB_storage object against the
Employees table
    $oEmp = new DB_storage( 'Employees', 'id', $oDB
);

    // create a new DB_storage object against the
EmployeesToDepartments table
    $oEmpToDept = new DB_storage(
'EmployeesToDepartments', array( 'emp_id',
'dept_id' ), $oDB );
```

Page 125

```
15        // initialize the employee object with the
       Employee whose id = 1
16        $oEmp->setup( 1 );
17
18        // initialize the employee-to-department object
       using emp_id = 1, dept_id = 2
19        $oEmpToDept->setup( array( 1, 2 ) );
20
21        print( 'Employee information: <br><br>' );
22        $oEmp->dump();
23
24        print( '<br>Employee-to-Department information:
       <br><br>' );
25        $oEmpToDept->dump();
26
27        $oDB->disconnect();
28    }
29    else
30    {
31      var_dump( $oDB );
32    }
33  ?>
```

Code Listing 61: Using setup().

The example shown in Code Listing 61 illustrates the use of the **setup()** method. Line 16 shows its use for a table with a single-column primary key. Line 19 shows its use with a table that has a two-column primary key. The output of the example is shown in Output 33.

```
1    Employee information:
2
3    id = 1
4    last_name = Schwendiman
5    first_name = Blake
6    phone_ext = 2204
7    mgr_id = 3
8    dept_id = 1
9
10   Employee-to-Department information:
11
12   emp_id = 1
13   dept_id = 2
14   date_xferred = 2002-07-19
```

Output 33: Output of setup() example.

There is a bug in the current implementation of the **setup()** method. If you look at the code (within the PEAR distribution), the very first line is the bug:

```
function setup($keyval)
{
  $qval = $this->_dbh->quote($keyval);
  ...
```

🐾 If you wish to use this class, you will likely need to comment out the first line of the **setup()** method. On investigation, this return value of this line, *qval*, is not used within the method and the quoting of the actual key values is done later in the method.

🐾 This bug has been reported to the PEAR::DB maintainers.

➲ Returns DB_OK on success or a DB_Error on failure.

DB_storage::insert

❖ *mixed* insert(*mixed* $newpk)

The **insert()** method is analogous to the INSERT SQL statement – a new row is created in the database with the primary key information specified by *newpk*.

The code in Code Listing 62 illustrates how to insert a new database record using the **insert()** method. After execution, a new row in the database exists assuming there was no primary key collision for the key specified on line 13.

```
1    <?php
2      error_reporting( E_ALL );
3      require_once( 'DB.php' );
4      require_once( 'DB/storage.php' );
5
6      $oDB = DB::connect(
       'mysql://bt_user:bt_pass@207.44.182.3/book_test',
       true );
7      if ( DB::isConnection( $oDB ) )
8      {
```

```
 9        // create a new DB_storage object against the
      Employees table
10        $oEmp = new DB_storage( 'Employees', 'id', $oDB
      );
11
12        // create a new Employee with ID = 50
13        $result = $oEmp->insert( 50 );
14
15        if ( !DB::isError( $result ) )
16        {
17           // set other Employee information with set()
      method
18           $oEmp->set( 'first_name', 'Jim' );
19           $oEmp->set( 'last_name', 'Murphy' );
20           $oEmp->set( 'mgr_id', 1 );
21           $oEmp->set( 'dept_id', 1 );
22
23           // save this object to the database
24           $oEmp->store();
25        }
26        else
27        {
28           var_dump( $result );
29        }
30
31        $oDB->disconnect();
32     }
33     else
34     {
35        var_dump( $oDB );
36     }
37  ?>
```

Code Listing 62: Using insert().

➲ Returns a DB_Error object on failure or NULL on success.

DB_storage::toString

❖ *string* toString(*void*)

The **toString()** method returns a short string describing the DB_storage object.

```
1  <?php
2     error_reporting( E_ALL );
3     require_once( 'DB.php' );
4     require_once( 'DB/storage.php' );
5
6     $oDB = DB::connect(
      'mysql://bt_user:bt_pass@207.44.182.3/book_test',
      true );
7     if ( DB::isConnection( $oDB ) )
8        {
```

```
9        // create a new DB_storage object against the
      Employees table
10       $oEmp = new DB_storage( 'Employees', 'id', $oDB
      );
11
12       // create a new Employee with ID = 50
13       $result = $oEmp->setup( 50 );
14
15       if ( !DB::isError( $result ) )
16       {
17         print( $oEmp->toString() );
18       }
19       else
20       {
21         var_dump( $result );
22       }
23
24       $oDB->disconnect();
25     }
26     else
27     {
28       var_dump( $oDB );
29     }
30   ?>
```

Code Listing 63: Using toString().

The output of Code Listing 63 is shown in Output 34.

```
1    db_storage (table=Employees, keycolumn=id,
     dbh=db_mysql: (phptype=mysql, dbsyntax=mysql)
     [connected]) [loaded, key=50]
```

Output 34: Output of DB_storage::toString().

➲ Returns a string.

DB_storage::dump

❖ *void* dump(*void*)

The **dump()** method dumps the properties of the DB_storage object to standard output. Standard output is the web browser output HTML stream when PHP is running in the context of a web server.

For a usage example, see Code Listing 60 on page 123.

➲ Returns no value but creates output on standard output.

DB_storage::create

❖ *object* create(*string* $table, *array* $data)

The internal documentation for the **create()** method indicates that **create()** is a static method used to create new DB_storage objects.

However, from my interpretation of the code inside the **create()** method, it does not appear that this method can be used statically (there is a reference to *$this*). Additionally, it appears that even if an object *could* be created it would not be sufficiently initialized to be useful.

🖎 I will accept comments regarding this method's use via the forums or personal messages at **http://www.intechra.net/**. Otherwise, I suggest avoiding this method entirely.

DB_storage::set

❖ *mixed* set(*string* $property, *mixed* $newvalue)

The **set()** method is the primary mechanism for updating properties of the DB_storage object which, in turn, update the columns of the database row represented by the object.

The **store()** method should typically be called to
realize any changes to the database, but it is important
to note that the DB_storage destructor will call the
store() procedure if there are any changes to the
object.

➲ Returns TRUE on success or a DB_Error object on
failure.

DB_storage::get

❖ mixed get(*string* $property)

The **get()** method fetches the current value of a
property of the object. If the named property does
not exist, **get()** returns NULL.

```php
<?php
   error_reporting( E_ALL );
   require_once( 'DB.php' );
   require_once( 'DB/storage.php' );

   function MyValidator( $sTable, $sProperty,
$mNewValue, $mOldValue, $oEmp )
   {
      print( "MyValidator( $sTable, $sProperty,
$mNewValue, $mOldValue, $oEmp )<br>" );

      if ( ( $sTable == 'Employees' ) && ( $sProperty
== 'phone_ext' ) )
      {
         // valid phone extensions range from 200 to
4999
         if ( ( $mNewValue >= 5000 ) || ( $mNewValue <
200 ) )
         {
            return false;
         }
      }

      return true;
   }

   $oDB = DB::connect(
'mysql://bt_user:bt_pass@207.44.182.3/book_test',
true );
   if ( DB::isConnection( $oDB ) )
   {
      // create a new DB_storage object against the
Employees table
      $aEmp = new DB_storage( 'Employees', 'id',
$oDB, 'MyValidator' );
```

```
28      // load the employee with ID = 1
29      $aEmp->setup( 1 );
30      $aEmp->dump();
31
32      // get a property
33      $iMgrId = $aEmp->get( 'mgr_id' );
34
35      if ( $iMgrId == 3 )
36      {
37          // set some properties
38          $aEmp->set( 'first_name', 'Joe' );
39          $aEmp->set( 'phone_ext', '9987' );
40
41          $aEmp->store();
42      }
43      $aEmp->dump();
44
45      $oDB->disconnect();
46   }
47   else
48   {
49       var_dump( $oDB );
50   }
51   ?>
```

Code Listing 64: Using set() and get().

The example in Code Listing 64 illustrates the use of both **set()** and **get()**. These methods are simple enough to understand.

Code Listing 64 also illustrates using a custom validation callback function to validate data provided through the **set()** method. The last argument to the DB_storage constructor (line 26) specifies the callback function for data validation. In this case, it is simply a function called *MyValidator*. It could be a method of a class, in which case it would be specified as an array containing the class name and method name as elements as with any callback function in PHP.

In the example, the validation function prints a line showing its arguments. It also validates any proposed changes to the *phone_ext* property to ensure that the new value falls within an acceptable range.

The output of the script is shown in Output 35.

```
1   id = 1
2   last_name = Schwendiman
3   first_name = Blake
4   phone_ext = 2204
5   mgr_id = 3
6   dept_id = 1
7   MyValidator( Employees, first_name, Joe, Blake,
    Object )
8   MyValidator( Employees, phone_ext, 9987, 2204,
    Object )
9   id = 1
10  last_name = Schwendiman
11  first_name = Joe
12  phone_ext = 2204
13  mgr_id = 3
14  dept_id = 1
```

Output 35: Using set() and get() and a callback validation function.

➲ Returns a property value which can be any atomic type or NULL.

DB_storage::store

❖ *mixed* store(*void*)

The **store()** method is called to realize any changes in the object to the database, but it is important to note that the DB_storage destructor will call the **store()** procedure if there are any changes to the object.

For an example of usage, see Code Listing 64 on page 132.

➲ Returns DB_OK or a DB_Error object.

DB_storage::remove

❖ *mixed* remove(*void*)

The **remove()** method actually removes the row of
data represented by the DB_storage object from the
database.

```
1   <?php
2     error_reporting( E_ALL );
3     require_once( 'DB.php' );
4     require_once( 'DB/storage.php' );
5
6     $oDB = DB::connect(
   'mysql://bt_user:bt_pass@207.44.182.3/book_test',
   true );
7     if ( DB::isConnection( $oDB ) )
8     {
9       // create a new DB_storage object against the
   Employees table
10      $aEmp = new DB_storage( 'Employees', 'id', $oDB
   );
11
12      $aEmp->setup( 50 );
13      $aEmp->remove();
14
15      $oDB->disconnect();
16    }
17    else
18    {
19      var_dump( $oDB );
20    }
21  ?>
```

Code Listing 65: Using remove().

The example in Code Listing 65 shows how to use
remove() to delete a row in the database.

➲ Returns DB_OK or a DB_Error object.

Database Support

PEAR::DB provides support for the databases listed
in Table 1 on page 19. This section of the book is
provided to show how a single script can be used to
access several database back ends while only changing
the DSN in the script.

Several factors are assumed in the example script. First, it is assumed that the database is running and PHP is configured with the appropriate code/drivers to access the database. Second, it is assumed that the user specified in the DSN has appropriate database privileges to perform the tasks in the script. Third, it is assumed that a database called *book_test* exists on the target database server. This section of the book is intended to primarily provide very high-level information about each of the supported databases and not to be a primer on installing and configuring each database. As appropriate, I may mention some interesting configuration or setup information identified in my testing. For the most part, this book was developed running PHP on Windows, so little of the database-specific information will be based on Linux (or other unix-like) operating systems.

The test program is divided into three files. The first file is the main script shown in Code Listing 66. The second file is the included file, *err_popup.php* which is just the functions from the example shown in Code Listing 20 on page 52. These functions popup a separate browser window and display the DB_Error object information. The third file (*db_specific.php*) is a set of database specific strings shown in Code Listing 67.

It should be obvious to any reader that not all SQL servers provide the same features or even the same syntax for SQL statements. The *db_specific.php* file contains those SQL statements that create the *Employees* table since table creation is typically very different between database servers. Other information stored in the *db_specific.php* file includes the DSN information and the full name of the database server for display.

The discussion of various parts of Code Listing 66 is given immediately below the listing itself.

```php
<?php
  $aInsertQueries[] = "INSERT INTO Employees VALUES
(1, 'Schwendiman', 'Joe', '2204', 3, 1)";
  $aInsertQueries[] = "INSERT INTO Employees VALUES
(2, 'Cox', 'Jeffrey', '225', 0, 1)";
  $aInsertQueries[] = "INSERT INTO Employees VALUES
(3, 'McNulty', 'Kate', '214', 3, 2)";
  $aInsertQueries[] = "INSERT INTO Employees VALUES
(4, 'Schwendiman', 'Ryan', '128', 1, 1)";
  $aInsertQueries[] = "INSERT INTO Employees VALUES
(51, 'Murphy', 'Jim', '', 1, 1)";
  $aInsertQueries[] = "INSERT INTO Employees VALUES
(58, 'Schwendiman', 'Scott', '234', 1, 1)";
  $aInsertQueries[] = "INSERT INTO Employees VALUES
(59, 'Schwendiman', 'Taylor', '323', 1, 1)";

  $aSelectQueries[] = "SELECT * from Employees
order by last_name, first_name";
  $aSelectQueries[] = "SELECT * from Employees
where ( mgr_id = 3 )";
  $aSelectQueries[] = "SELECT * from Employees
where ( dept_id = 2 )";

  $aUpdateQueries[] = "UPDATE Employees set mgr_id
= 2 where ( mgr_id = 3 )";
  $aUpdateQueries[] = "UPDATE Employees set dept_id
= 3 where ( mgr_id = 2 )";

  $aDeleteQueries[] = "DELETE FROM Employees where
( phone_ext < 300 )";
?>

<!DOCTYPE HTML PUBLIC "-//W3C//DTD HTML 4.0
Transitional//EN">

<html>
<head>
        <title>PEAR::DB General Test</title>
</head>

<body>

<?php
  error_reporting( E_ALL );
  require_once( 'DB.php' );
  require_once( 'err_popup.php' );
  require_once( 'db_specific.php' );

  $sDBType = 'mssql';

  function DisplayHeader( $aRow )
  {
    print( '<tr>' );
    print( '<td> </td>' );
    foreach ( $aRow as $aName => $aValue )
    {
```

```
43        print( '<td>' . $aName . '</td>' );
44      }
45      print( '</tr>' );
46    }
47
48    function DisplayResults( $oResult )
49    {
50      print( 'Number of rows in query result = <b>' .
    $oResult->numRows() . '</b><br><br>' );
51
52      if ( $oResult->numRows() > 0 )
53      {
54        print( '<table border="1" width="90%"
    align="center">' );
55        $iResultNum = 0;
56        while ( $aRow = $oResult->fetchRow() )
57        {
58          if ( $iResultNum == 0 )
59            DisplayHeader( $aRow );
60
61          print( '<tr>' );
62          print( '<td>' . $iResultNum . '</td>' );
63          foreach ( $aRow as $aValue )
64          {
65            print( '<td>' . $aValue . '</td>' );
66          }
67          print( '</tr>' );
68          $iResultNum++;
69        }
70        print( '</table><br>' );
71      }
72    }
73
74    function DoSelectQueries( $oDB )
75    {
76      global $aSelectQueries;
77
78      foreach ( $aSelectQueries as $sSQL )
79      {
80        print( 'Executing query: <i>' . $sSQL .
    '</i><br><br>' );
81        $result = $oDB->query( $sSQL );
82        if ( !DB::isError( $result ) )
83        {
84          DisplayResults( $result );
85          $result->free();
86        }
87        else
88        {
89          errorPopup( $result );
90          exit;
91        }
92      }
93    }
94
95    print( 'Running PEAR::DB test for database ' .
    $aDBPrettyNames[$sDBType] . '<br><br>' );
96
97    $sDSN = $aDSNValues[$sDBType];
98    $oDB  = DB::connect( $sDSN, true );
99    if ( DB::isConnection( $oDB ) )
100   {
101     $oDB->setFetchMode( DB_FETCHMODE_ASSOC );
```

```
102
103     // try to get the current list of tables for
    this database
104     $result = $oDB->getTables();
105     if ( !DB::isError( $result ) )
106     {
107       print( 'Tables currently in database:<ol>' );
108       foreach ( $result as $sTable )
109       {
110         print( '<li>' . $sTable . '</li>' );
111       }
112       print( '</ol>' );
113
114       // delete the Employees table if it exists
115       if ( in_array( 'Employees', $result ) )
116       {
117         $sSQL = 'DROP TABLE Employees';
118         $result = $oDB->query( $sSQL );
119         if ( DB::isError( $result ) )
120         {
121           errorPopup( $result );
122           exit;
123         }
124
125         print( 'Employees table successfully
    dropped.<br><br>' );
126       }
127     }
128     else
129     {
130       errorPopup( $result );
131       exit;
132     }
133
134     // create the Employees table on the database
135     foreach ( $aCreateTableCmds[$sDBType] as $sSQL
    )
136     {
137       $result = $oDB->query( $sSQL );
138       if ( DB::isError( $result ) )
139       {
140         errorPopup( $result );
141         exit;
142       }
143     }
144     print( 'Employees table successfully
    created.<br><br>' );
145
146     // populate the Table with some data
147     foreach ( $aInsertQueries as $sSQL )
148     {
149       $result = $oDB->query( $sSQL );
150       if ( DB::isError( $result ) )
151       {
152         errorPopup( $result );
153         exit;
154       }
155     }
156     print( 'All data inserted
    successfully.<br><br>' );
157
158     DoSelectQueries( $oDB );
159
```

```
160      foreach ( $aUpdateQueries as $sSQL )
161      {
162        $result = $oDB->query( $sSQL );
163        if ( DB::isError( $result ) )
164        {
165          errorPopup( $result );
166          exit;
167        }
168      }
169      print( 'All update queries finished
         successfully.<br><br>' );
170
171      DoSelectQueries( $oDB );
172
173      foreach ( $aDeleteQueries as $sSQL )
174      {
175        $result = $oDB->query( $sSQL );
176        if ( DB::isError( $result ) )
177        {
178          errorPopup( $result );
179          exit;
180        }
181      }
182      print( 'All delete queries finished
         successfully.<br><br>' );
183
184      DoSelectQueries( $oDB );
185
186      $oDB->disconnect();
187    }
188    else
189    {
190      errorPopup( $oDB );
191    }
192 ?>
193
194 </body>
195 </html>
196
```

Code Listing 66: General PEAR::DB test script (main).

Lines 2 – 17 of the script set up some arrays of SQL statements that are not database specific that are used in the script later.

Starting on line 95, the script first obtains the database-specific DSN and attempts to connect to the database. If the connection is successful, the database object's *fetchmode* is set to DB_FETCHMODE_ASSOC.

Next, in lines 103 – 132, the current list of tables in the database is retrieved and displayed. If a table exists with the name *Employees*, it is dropped.

Next, the *Employees* table is created using the database-specific creation SQL statements in lines 134 – 144. Rows of data are then added to the table in lines 146 – 156.

On line 158, the **DoSelectQueries()** function is called. The **DoSelectQueries()** function is internal to this script and does some interesting work. The source for the function is listed in lines 74 – 93. For each of the SQL queries in the *$aSelectQueries* array, the query is execute and the result (if not an error) is passed to the **DisplayResults()** function. The **DisplayResults()** function displays the number of rows in the result set, then if the number of rows is more than 0, it loops through the results using the **fetchRow()** method. On the first iteration of the loop, the **DisplayHeader()** function is called which displays the column names of the result set in an HTML table. This is a nice workaround to the problem that not all database back ends provide an implementation of the **tableInfo()** method. Then the data itself is displayed as the **fetchRow()** loop continues.

After the initial data is populated and displayed, the script then runs a set of update queries in lines 160 – 169. The **DoSelectQueries()** function is called again to display the data in the table.

Finally, the script runs a set of delete queries in lines 173 – 182 and the results are again displayed.

```
1    <?php
```

```
2     $aDBPrettyNames ['mssql'] = 'Microsoft SQL
      Server';
3     $aDSNValues      ['mssql'] =
      'mssql://user:pass@dbserver/book_test';
4     $aCreateTableCmds['mssql'] = array( 'CREATE TABLE
      [dbo].[Employees] ( [id] [int] NOT NULL ,
      [last_name] [char] (50) COLLATE
      SQL_Latin1_General_CP1_CI_AS NULL , [first_name]
      [char] (50) COLLATE SQL_Latin1_General_CP1_CI_AS
      NULL , [phone_ext] [char] (5) COLLATE
      SQL_Latin1_General_CP1_CI_AS NULL , [mgr_id] [int]
      NULL , [dept_id] [int] NULL ) ON [PRIMARY]',
5                                          'ALTER TABLE
      [dbo].[Employees] WITH NOCHECK ADD CONSTRAINT
      [PK_Employees] PRIMARY KEY  CLUSTERED ( [id] )  ON
      [PRIMARY] ' );
6
7     $aDBPrettyNames ['mysql']   = 'MySQL';
8     $aDSNValues      ['mysql']   =
      'mysql://bt_user:bt_pass@207.44.182.3/book_test';
9     $aCreateTableCmds['mysql'][] = "CREATE TABLE
      Employees ( id int(11) NOT NULL default '0',
      last_name varchar(50) NOT NULL default '',
      first_name varchar(50) NOT NULL default '',
      phone_ext varchar(5) NOT NULL default '', mgr_id
      int(11) NOT NULL default '0', dept_id int(11) NOT
      NULL default '0', PRIMARY KEY  (id), KEY mgr_id
      (mgr_id), KEY dept_id (dept_id) ) TYPE=InnoDB";
10
11    $aDBPrettyNames ['odbc']    = 'ODBC with Access
      DB';
12    $aDSNValues      ['odbc']    =
      'odbc://book_test';
13    $aCreateTableCmds['odbc'][]   = 'CREATE TABLE
      [Employees] ( [id] integer NOT NULL , [last_name]
      char(50) NULL, [first_name] char(50) NULL,
      [phone_ext] char(5) NULL, [mgr_id] integer NULL ,
      [dept_id] integer NULL )';
14    $aCreateTableCmds['odbc'][]   = 'ALTER TABLE
      [Employees]  ADD CONSTRAINT [PK_Employees] PRIMARY
      KEY  ( [id] )';
15
16    $aDBPrettyNames ['sqlite']   = 'SQLite';
17    $aDSNValues      ['sqlite']   =
      'sqlite:///c:/temp/PEAR/sqlite_employees.dat';
18    $aCreateTableCmds['sqlite'][]   = 'CREATE TABLE
      Employees ( id [integer] NOT NULL PRIMARY KEY,
      last_name [char(50)], first_name [char(50)],
      phone_ext [char(5)], mgr_id [integer], dept_id
      [integer] )';
19
20    $aDBPrettyNames ['ibase']    = 'Borland
      Interbase';
21    $aDSNValues      ['ibase']    =
      'ibase://sysdba:masterkey@localhost/c:/temp/PEAR/bo
      ok_test.gdb';
22    $aCreateTableCmds['ibase'][]   = 'CREATE TABLE
      Employees ( id integer NOT NULL PRIMARY KEY,
      last_name char(50), first_name char(50), phone_ext
      char(5), mgr_id integer, dept_id integer )';
23
24    $aDBPrettyNames ['msql']     = 'Mini SQL';
```

```
25    $aDSNValues        ['msql']      =
      'msql://msql.server.example.com/book_test';
26    $aCreateTableCmds['msql'][]   = 'CREATE TABLE
      Employees ( id integer NOT NULL PRIMARY KEY,
      last_name char(50), first_name char(50), phone_ext
      char(5), mgr_id integer, dept_id integer )';
27
28
29    $aDBPrettyNames   ['fbsql']    = 'FrontBase';
30    $aDSNValues       ['fbsql']    =
      'fbsql://bt_user@localhost/book_test';
31    $aCreateTableCmds['fbsql'][]  = 'CREATE TABLE
      Employees ( id integer NOT NULL PRIMARY KEY,
      last_name char(50), first_name char(50), phone_ext
      char(5), mgr_id integer, dept_id integer )';
32
33    $aDBPrettyNames   ['ifx']      = 'Informix';
34    $aDSNValues       ['ifx']      =
      'ifx://informix:informix@ol_matt/book_test';
35    $aCreateTableCmds['ifx'][]     = 'CREATE TABLE
      Employees ( id integer NOT NULL PRIMARY KEY,
      last_name char(50), first_name char(50), phone_ext
      char(5), mgr_id integer, dept_id integer )';
36
37    $aDBPrettyNames   ['pgsql']    = 'PostgreSQL';
38    $aDSNValues       ['pgsql']    =
      'pgsql://blake:password@pgsql.server.example.com/bo
      ok_test';
39    $aCreateTableCmds['pgsql'][]   = 'CREATE TABLE
      Employees ( id integer NOT NULL PRIMARY KEY,
      last_name char(50), first_name char(50), phone_ext
      char(5), mgr_id integer, dept_id integer )';
40    ?>
```

Code Listing 67: Source of *db_specific.php* – Database Specific Code

The following is the output of the script for the Microsoft SQL Server database. It represents the baseline output for the test. In the database-specific sections below, only deviances from this baseline will be noted.

```
Running PEAR::DB test for database Microsoft
SQL Server

Tables currently in database:

1.  dtproperties
2.  Employees
```

```
Employees table successfully dropped.

Employees table successfully created.

All data inserted successfully.

Executing query: SELECT * from Employees
order by last_name, first_name

Number of rows in query result = 7
```

	id	last_name	first_n ame	phone _ext	mgr _id	dept _id
0	2	Cox	Jeffrey	225	0	1
1	3	McNulty	Kate	214	3	2
2	51	Murphy	Jim		1	1
3	1	Schwendi man	Joe	2204	3	1
4	4	Schwendi man	Ryan	128	1	1
5	58	Schwendi man	Scott	234	1	1
6	59	Schwendi man	Taylor	323	1	1

```
Executing query: SELECT * from Employees
where ( mgr_id = 3 )

Number of rows in query result = 2
```

	id	last_name	first_name	phone_ext	mgr_id	dept_id
0	1	Schwendiman	Joe	2204	3	1
1	3	McNulty	Kate	214	3	2

```
Executing query: SELECT * from Employees
where ( dept_id = 2 )

Number of rows in query result = 1
```

	i d	last_na me	first_na me	phone_ ext	mgr_ id	dept_ id
0	3	McNult	Kate	214	3	2

		y				

All update queries finished successfully.

Executing query: *SELECT * from Employees order by last_name, first_name*

Number of rows in query result = **7**

	id	last_name	first_name	phone_ext	mgr_id	dept_id
0	2	Cox	Jeffrey	225	0	1
1	3	McNulty	Kate	214	2	3
2	51	Murphy	Jim		1	1
3	1	Schwendiman	Joe	2204	2	3
4	4	Schwendiman	Ryan	128	1	1
5	58	Schwendiman	Scott	234	1	1
6	59	Schwendiman	Taylor	323	1	1

Executing query: *SELECT * from Employees where (mgr_id = 3)*

Number of rows in query result = **0**

Executing query: *SELECT * from Employees where (dept_id = 2)*

Number of rows in query result = **0**

All delete queries finished successfully.

Executing query: *SELECT * from Employees order by last_name, first_name*

Number of rows in query result = **2**

	id	last_name	first_name	phone_ext	mgr_id	dept_id
0	1	Schwendi	Joe	2204	2	3

		man				
1	5 9	Schwendi man	Taylor	323	1	1

```
Executing query: SELECT * from Employees
where ( mgr_id = 3 )

Number of rows in query result = 0

Executing query: SELECT * from Employees
where ( dept_id = 2 )

Number of rows in query result = 0
```

The output shown above has been slightly reformatted for readability, but provides the information needed.

MySQL

MySQL is likely to be the most commonly-used database for PHP programmers. All versions of PHP 4 enable built-in support for MySQL databases. For either the Windows or unix-like platforms, MySQL support is typically on by default.

The DSN format for MySQL is illustrated in most of the examples in this book. The most common DSN format for a MySQL database is likely to be:

```
1    phptype://username:password@hostspec/database_name
```

The *hostspec* portion can contain just a hostname or IP address, or a *host:port* formatted host specification.

The general test script shown above worked without any problems for my MySQL installation (*MySQL 4.0.15-Max*).

PostgreSQL

The support for PostgreSQL in PHP and PEAR::DB is excellent. The test example worked for PostgreSQL with only a minor change. The "DROP TABLE" command needs to be altered for a lower-case table name. Again, my inexperience with the database may be part of the problem. In any case, experienced PostgreSQL users will know the particulars of the database and avoid such bugs.

Borland Interbase

Borland Interbase is supported by PHP in general, but I was unable to get the PEAR test to run successfully.

First, the **getTables()** method is not supported in the PEAR::DB implementation for Interbase, so the code had to be reworked. There is a sample script (available with the source code at **http://www.intechra.net/**) called *code_listing_67.php* that removes the lines related to the **getTables()** method.

After getting the script to run past the initial **getTables()** failure, I encountered a consistent error in a select SQL statement:

```
1    Running PEAR::DB test for database Borland
     Interbase
2
3    Employees table successfully dropped.
4
5    Employees table successfully created.
6
```

```
7    All data inserted successfully.
8
9    Executing query: SELECT * from Employees order by
     last_name, first_name
10
11   Number of rows in query result = Object
12
13
14   Executing query: SELECT * from Employees where (
     mgr_id = 3 )
15
16   PHP has encountered an Access Violation at 77F83AED
```

The error on line 16 occurred in every test run. After getting the error, it was necessary to stop and restart IIS.

Without jumping to any conclusions, I have to assume that my configuration is not correct for using PHP with Interbase. Assuming a correctly-running PHP + Interbase configuration, I also have to assume that the PEAR::DB test above will work correctly, save for the missing implementation for **getTables()**.

Mini SQL

Apparently I'm not intelligent enough to get Mini SQL to work correctly. I was entirely unable to use a Windows PHP installation to connect to a remote Linux-based Mini SQL server. I followed every step on the **http://www.php.net/msql** page, but to no avail. I was able to eventually establish a connection from PHP when I switched to using PHP + Mini SQL on Linux. However, the test code failed to run at various different places (each run seemed to fail at a different spot).

Many of the links on the Mini SQL home page are broken (especially related to Windows support), so I am left to make some assumptions about the general state of the project.

My suggestion to a PHP developer looking for a small database backend is to check out SQLite. I had no problems setting it up and there were no problems with the PEAR::DB test code.

Microsoft SQL Server

Microsoft SQL Server is extremely simple to set up in a Windows-based PHP install. For testing, I simply installed the latest PHP binaries available from the PHP web site. After configuring PHP at the most basic level to begin testing, it is necessary to load the MS SQL extension by editing the *php.ini* file.

Simply remove the semicolon comment character preceding the line '*extension=php_mssql.dll*' in the configuration file and it works.

Configuration of non-Windows PHP for use with a MS SQL database is slightly more complicated, but still possible. See **http://www.php.net/mssql** for setup instructions.

Once running, PHP works great with MS SQL server and the PEAR::DB implementation is very complete. The test script works perfectly for MS SQL server as tested against MS SQL Server 2000 (version 8.00.760 SP3).

Oracle 7/8/8i

Unfortunately I was unable to get a fully-functioning test Oracle database running. I have used Oracle with PHP in the past and I found its support to be adequate for the tasks at that time.

ODBC

It is difficult the generalize anything about the ODBC support in PEAR::DB. That is because ODBC can mean so many things. In PHP, the ODBC driver can be used to provide native access to Adabas D, IBM DB2, iODBC, Solid, and Sybase SQL Anywhere databases. It can also provide generic ODBC access to any number of databases on a Windows platform or remote ODBC access to databases using the ODBC-ODBC bridge product available on Windows and Linux.

For the purposes of this book, I set up a MS Access database and created a Windows DSN through which the ODBC driver was able to connect to Access. Generally this scenario works. However, there are problems with the general test script. The ODBC object does not support the **getTables()** method. Therefore, the test script failed early on trying to determine whether the *Employees* database existed. After re-working the script to ignore the errors associated with the **getTables()** method, the script ran successfully against a MS Access database.

Again, it is very important to note that ODBC has such a broad meaning in the PHP world so it is virtually impossible to generalize how well PEAR::DB will work with an ODBC-based server.

SyBase

Unfortunately I was unable to get SyBase running correctly for my testing.

Informix

The PEAR::DB example script used throughout this section just didn't work with Informix. Without doing a great deal of research into the exact nature of the errors, I simply found that the required calls did not exist or work the same way for the Informix object.

My configuration was the Informix Dynamic Server running on Windows XP. The client tools were also installed and running on the same machine. The PHP and web server were also on the same machine. While I was able to connect to the database and create the *Employees* table, there were problems later in obtaining the results. The **getTables()** method was not supported.

Again, in this case, I accept the fact that my experience configuring and using Informix with PHP is the primary culprit. Any suggestions can be sent to me via my contact information at http://www.intechra.net/.

FrontBase

FrontBase support in PHP is excellent. Within 10 minutes I was able to download, install and configure FrontBase on my Windows XP machine. I was also able to locate and download the extension DLL, '*php_fbsql.dll*' and configure PHP via the *php.ini* file to use FrontBase. The general PEAR::DB test script ran without any trouble the first time it was tried.

Considering that I have had no previous experience with FrontBase, this is very encouraging. If you are considering using FrontBase with your PHP application, there are a development licenses available so you can test your application before making the financial commitment to deploy.

SQLite

SQLite is an interesting database engine that will be shipping (according to recent online sources) with PHP by default starting in version 5 of PHP. SQLite is a file-based database engine that is (as its name implies) very lightweight. The DSN specification is something like:

```
1    sqlite:///c:/temp/PEAR/sqlite_employees.dat
```

The above DSN works on Windows, but it can be simply adapted for use on other operating systems by simply updating the path format appropriately.

Installing SQLite on a Windows-based PHP is a snap. Simply download the *php_sqlite.dll* file available from **http://www.php.net/sqlite** and then download the actual SQLite engine DLL (*sqlite.dll*) from the SQLite web site at **http://www.sqlite.org/**. Place the *sqlite.dll* file in the search path of Windows (such as the *system32* directory), then copy *php_sqlite.dll* to your PHP extensions directory. Then enable SQLite by adding '*extension=php_sqlite.dll*' to your *php.ini* file.

The test script runs without any errors or warnings. There is, however, a single notice generated:

```
1    Notice: Undefined index: mode in C:\temp\PEAR\php-
     4.3.4-Win32\pear\DB\sqlite.php on line 185
```

This warning is based on the fact that for some reason, the SQLite database object expects the parsed DSN to have a member called *mode* which does not exist. Perhaps this will be added in a future version of PEAR::DB. In any case, this notice will not be displayed if you are running in a typically configured environment. However, if you are running SQLite on a unix-like operating system, the *mode* value specifies the file mode (e.g. 0644) which you may wish to specify. If you do, you will need to edit the DB_sqlite implementation or use an array-based DSN and provide the *mode* key directly.

The SQLite support in PEAR::DB is surprisingly complete for such a new database (from the PHP perspective). Using SQLite may be preferred in restricted hosting environments or in situations where a full database backend is not required. The overhead of SQLite is very small and the SQL language support is very complete.

dBase

dBase support in PEAR::DB is extremely limited. The example code will not work with dBase because so little of the interface is truly supported. After looking a bit on the PHP web site, even dBase itself is not fully supported:

> There is no support for indexes or memo fields. There is no support for locking, too. Two concurrent

webserver processes modifying the same dBase file will very likely ruin your database.

...

We recommend that you do not use dBase files as your production database. Choose any real SQL server instead; MySQL or Postgres are common choices with PHP. dBase support is here to allow you to import and export data to and from your web database, because the file format is commonly understood by Windows spreadsheets and organizers.

Clearly dBase support is provided at the most basic level for PHP programmers, therefore PEAR::DB support is also limited.

Database Support Summary

After having testing PEAR::DB with most of the backend databases that it supports, I would make the following recommendations. First, PEAR::DB support is intrinsically related to the level of PHP support for the backend. For example, the support for dBase in PHP is limited, so naturally, the support for dBase in PEAR::DB is also limited.

Next, SQL support varies between the backend databases. Complete database portability is unlikely since the SQL syntax is so variable.

Lastly, there are simply some database back ends that are more used by the PHP community at large, so their support is likely to always be better. In my testing, it became clear that MySQL, PostreSQL, Microsoft SQL Server, FrontBase and SQLite have the most mature PHP support.

Conclusion

PEAR::DB is a powerful, object-oriented abstraction layer that is supported and maintained by members of the core PHP development team. PEAR::DB is the right tool for any database-enabled PHP application, no matter its size. The primary reasons to use PEAR::DB are to enable rapid (or more rapid) application development and application maintainability through code reuse. While PEAR::DB can enable database portability, most medium to large applications will rely on the underlying database to the point that engine-specific SQL will likely be used.

As PHP matures, so will PEAR::DB. Developers serious about maintainability of their applications over the long-term should seriously consider PEAR::DB as their database abstraction layer.

Appendix A: Lists of Figures

Tables

TABLE 1: PEAR::DB SUPPORTED DATABASES 19
TABLE 2: DEFAULT OPTIONS FOR DATABASE CLASSES 20
TABLE 3: DB CLASS METHODS 30
TABLE 4: DSN ARRAY ELEMENTS 36
TABLE 5: RESULTS OF CODE LISTING 18 (RE-FORMATTED FOR BOOK) 46
TABLE 6: PLACEHOLDER CHARACTERS FOR USE IN QUERY() METHOD 60
TABLE 7: TYPES SUPPORTED IN GETSPECIALQUERY FOR EACH DATABASE BACK END. 107
TABLE 8: DB_RESULT CLASS METHODS 109
TABLE 9: DB_STORAGE CLASS METHODS 125

Figures

FIGURE 1: SYSTEM PROPERTIES PAGE 4
FIGURE 2: ENVIRONMENT VARIABLES DIALOG 5
FIGURE 3: ADDING THE PATH TO THE PEAR.BAT FILE 5
FIGURE 4: POPUP WINDOW CREATED BY ERRORPOPUP FUNCTION 52
FIGURE 5: BROWSER-BASED OUTPUT OF CODE LISTING 58. . 117
FIGURE 6: OUTPUT OF DB_STORAGE OVERVIEW CODE. 124

Code Listings

CODE LISTING 1: MYSQL STATEMENTS TO CREATE SAMPLE DATABASE 10
CODE LISTING 2: SQL QUERY FOR SAMPLE EMPLOYEE DATABASE 11
CODE LISTING 3: PROCEDURAL DB ACCESS 12
CODE LISTING 4: PEAR::DB DATABASE ACCESS 13

CODE LISTING 5: PEAR::DB DATABASE ACCESS (TAKE TWO) 16

CODE LISTING 6: FULL DSN FORMAT 18

CODE LISTING 7: VARIATIONS OF DSN FORMAT 18

CODE LISTING 8: EXAMPLES OF DB::CONNECT() 22

CODE LISTING 9: USING SEQUENCES 23

CODE LISTING 10: CUSTOM SEQUENCE TABLE NAME FORMAT 25

CODE LISTING 11: OVERVIEW OF USING PREPARE() AND EXECUTE() 27

CODE LISTING 12: USING AUTOPREPARE 28

CODE LISTING 13: DB::FACTORY 32

CODE LISTING 14: SEVERAL EXAMPLES OF DB::CONNECT 34

CODE LISTING 15: DB::ASSERTEXTENSION EXAMPLE 37

CODE LISTING 16: DB_COMMON::TOSTRING EXAMPLE 42

CODE LISTING 17: DB_COMMON::QUOTE EXAMPLE 43

CODE LISTING 18: DB_COMMON::PROVIDES EXAMPLE 45

CODE LISTING 19: DB_COMMON::ERRORCODE, DB_COMMON::ERRORMESSAGE, DB_COMMON::ERRORNATIVE() EXAMPLE 47

CODE LISTING 20: USING DB_ERROR 52

CODE LISTING 21: DB_COMMON::SETFETCHMODE – DB_FETCHMODE_ORDERED (DEFAULT) 53

CODE LISTING 22: DB_COMMON::SETFETCHMODE – DB_FETCHMODE_ASSOC 55

CODE LISTING 23: DB_COMMON::SETFETCHMODE – DB_FETCHMODE_OBJECT 56

CODE LISTING 24: DB_COMMON::SETFETCHMODE – DB_FETCHMODE_OBJECT USING OBJECT_CLASS PARAMETER 58

CODE LISTING 25: USING PREPARE() -- SIMPLE EXAMPLE 61

CODE LISTING 26: SQL STATEMENTS FOR CREATING THE UPLOADEDFILES TABLE 62

CODE LISTING 27: THE PREPARE() METHOD USING THE '&' PLACEHOLDER 63

CODE LISTING 28: USING AUTOPREPARE() – INSERT 64

CODE LISTING 29: USING AUTOPREPARE() – UPDATE 65

CODE LISTING 30: USING AUTOEXECUTE() 67

CODE LISTING 31: USING BUILDMANIPSQL() 68

CODE LISTING 32: EXAMPLE OF EXECUTEEMULATEQUERY() 70

CODE LISTING 33: USING EXECUTEMULTIPLE() 71

CODE LISTING 34: USING QUERY() 73

CODE LISTING 35: LIMITING A MYSQL QUERY USING SQL ... 74

CODE LISTING 36: USING LIMITQUERY(). 76

CODE LISTING 37: USING GETONE(). 77

CODE LISTING 38: USING GETROW()..................................... 78

CODE LISTING 39: USING GETCOL()...................................... 80

CODE LISTING 40: USING GETASSOC() – SIMPLEST USAGE. ... 82

CODE LISTING 41: USING GETASSOC() – EXAMPLE WITH
SETFETCHMODE(). 84

CODE LISTING 42: USING GETASSOC() – ILLUSTRATING
FORCE_ARRAY PARAMETER (SET TO *FALSE*). 85

CODE LISTING 43: USING GETASSOC() – ILLUSTRATING
FORCE_ARRAY PARAMETER (SET TO *TRUE*)..................... 86

CODE LISTING 44: USING GETASSOC() – ILLUSTRATING *GROUP*
PARAMETER (SET TO *FALSE*). 87

CODE LISTING 45: USING GETASSOC() – ILLUSTRATING *GROUP*
PARAMETER (SET TO *TRUE*). 88

CODE LISTING 46: USING GETALL() – SIMPLEST USAGE. 90

CODE LISTING 47: USING GETALL() – USING
DB_FETCHMODE_FLIPPED.. 92

CODE LISTING 48: USING COMMIT()..................................... 94

CODE LISTING 49: USING ROLLBACK()................................... 97

CODE LISTING 50: USING NUMROWS()................................... 99

CODE LISTING 51: USING AFFECTEDROWS(). 100

CODE LISTING 52: USING CREATESEQUENCE() WITH MYSQL.
.... 102

CODE LISTING 53: USING TABLEINFO().............................. 103

CODE LISTING 54: USING GETTABLES(). 105

CODE LISTING 55: USING GETLISTOF()............................... 108

CODE LISTING 56: USING FETCHROW() WITH A SPECIFIED
ROWNUM. 112

CODE LISTING 57: USING FETCHINTO().............................. 113

CODE LISTING 58: USING TABLEINFO(). 117

CODE LISTING 59: THE *MODE* PARAMETER OF THE TABLEINFO()
METHOD... 118

CODE LISTING 60: OVERVIEW OF THE DB_STORAGE CLASS.123

CODE LISTING 61: USING SETUP(). 126

CODE LISTING 62: USING INSERT()..................................... 128

CODE LISTING 63: USING TOSTRING(). 129

CODE LISTING 64: USING SET() AND GET()........................... 132

CODE LISTING 65: USING REMOVE(). 134

CODE LISTING 66: GENERAL PEAR::DB TEST SCRIPT (MAIN).
.... 139

CODE LISTING 67: SOURCE OF *DB_SPECIFIC.PHP* – DATABASE
SPECIFIC CODE 142

Output Listings

OUTPUT 1: RUNNING THE PEAR COMMAND WITH NO
COMMAND-LINE ARGUMENTS 7
OUTPUT 2: OUTPUT OF PEAR LIST 7
OUTPUT 3: RESULTS OF SEQUENCE EXAMPLE (CODE LISTING 9)
.... 24
OUTPUT 4: RESULTS OF 2ND RUN OF SEQUENCE EXAMPLE.... 24
OUTPUT 5: DB::ASSERTEXTENSION EXAMPLE OUTPUT 37
OUTPUT 6: DB_COMMON::TOSTRING OUTPUT....................... 42
OUTPUT 7: DB_COMMON::QUOTE EXAMPLE OUTPUT............ 44
OUTPUT 8: OUTPUT WHEN SETFETCHMODE IS
DB_FETCHMODE_ORDERED................................ 54
OUTPUT 9: OUTPUT WHEN SETFETCHMODE IS
DB_FETCHMODE_ASSOC..................................... 55
OUTPUT 10: OUTPUT WHEN SETFETCHMODE IS
DB_FETCHMODE_OBJECT 56
OUTPUT 11: OUTPUT WHEN SETFETCHMODE IS
DB_FETCHMODE_OBJECT AND *OBJECT_CLASS* IS SET
.... 58
OUTPUT 12: EXAMPLES OF USING BUILDMANIPSQL().......... 68
OUTPUT 13: OUTPUT OF EXECUTEEMULATEQUERY() EXAMPLE
.... 70
OUTPUT 14: OUTPUT OF THE GETROW() METHOD. 79
OUTPUT 15: OUTPUT OF THE GETCOL() METHOD. 81
OUTPUT 16: OUTPUT OF GETASSOC() RELATED TO CODE
LISTING 40.. 83
OUTPUT 17: OUTPUT OF GETASSOC() RELATED TO CODE
LISTING 41.. 84
OUTPUT 18: OUTPUT OF GETASSOC() RELATED TO CODE
LISTING 42.. 85
OUTPUT 19: OUTPUT OF GETASSOC() RELATED TO CODE
LISTING 43.. 86
OUTPUT 20: OUTPUT OF GETASSOC() RELATED TO CODE
LISTING 44.. 88
OUTPUT 21: OUTPUT OF GETASSOC() RELATED TO CODE
LISTING 45.. 89
OUTPUT 22: OUTPUT OF GETALL() RELATED TO CODE LISTING
46. 91

OUTPUT 23: OUTPUT OF GETALL() RELATED TO CODE LISTING
    47. 93

OUTPUT 24: EXAMPLE OF USING COMMIT(). 96

OUTPUT 25: EXAMPLE OF USING ROLLBACK(). 98

OUTPUT 26: OUTPUT OF CREATESEQUENCE() ON MYSQL
    DATABASE WITH INSUFFICIENT USER PRIVILEGES. 102

OUTPUT 27: OUTPUT OF THE TABLEINFO() METHOD. 104

OUTPUT 28: OUTPUT RELATED TO GETTABLES EXAMPLE (CODE
    LISTING 54). 106

OUTPUT 29: OUTPUT OF THE GETLISTOF() EXAMPLE (CODE
    LISTING 55). 108

OUTPUT 30: RESULTS OF FETCHROW() FROM CODE LISTING 56.
    112

OUTPUT 31: RESULTS OF FETCHINTO EXAMPLE (CODE LISTING
    57). 114

OUTPUT 32: THE *MODE* PARAMETER OF THE TABLEINFO()
    METHOD. 120

OUTPUT 33: OUTPUT OF SETUP() EXAMPLE. 126

OUTPUT 34: OUTPUT OF DB_STORAGE::TOSTRING(). 129

OUTPUT 35: USING SET() AND GET() AND A CALLBACK
    VALIDATION FUNCTION. 133

Index

!

! 60

$

$_FILES 63

&

& 60

?

? 60

A

abstract 38
aggregate SQL function 76
ALTER 35

C

CREATE 35

D

Data Source Name .. 14, 17
database 36
databases 106
DB_FETCHMODE_ASS
  OC 53
DB_FETCHMODE_FLIP
  PED 53, 59, 91, 92
DB_FETCHMODE_OBJ
  ECT. 53, 55, 56, 57, 58,
  110
DB_FETCHMODE_ORD
  ERED 53
dBase 15, 19, 152, 153
dbsyntax 36
DELETE 35, 100
DROP 35
DSN 32

E

error handling 47
errorPopup 48
escapes 43
execute 26

F

file uploading 63
FrontBase . vi, 15, 19, 142,
  151, 154

G

go-pear.bat 2, 3
GRANT 35

H

hostspec 36
HTML table 117, 140

I

Informix .... vi, 14, 18, 142,
  150
INNODB 95
INSERT 35, 100
Installing PEAR 2
Interbase . v, 142, 146, 147

L

limit 44
limited query 74
LOCK 35

M

metadata 103
Microsoft SQL Server . 14,
  18, 141, 142, 143, 148,
  154
Mini SQL 14, 18, 142,
  147, 148

multiple result sets 115
multiple-field key 10
MySQL 145

N

native DB error 46

O

ODBC .. 14, 15, 16, 17, 18,
    43, 44, 141, 149, 150
Oracle .... v, 14, 18, 23, 25,
    149

P

pagination 76
password 36
pconnect 44
PEAR package manager 2,
    6, 7
pear.bat 3, 5
persistent connection ... 20,
    21, 22, 23, 25, 26, 33
PHP 5 69
PHP extension 30, 36
phptype 36
port 36
PostgreSQL 14, 18, 146
prepare 26, 44
protocol 36

Q

quotes 43

R

REPLACE 35
REVOKE 35

S

schema 106
sequence 101
Sequences 23
socket 36
SQLite ... 15, 19, 141, 148,
    151, 152, 154
stdClass object 57
SyBase 14, 18, 150

T

tables 106
transactions 44, 45, 93, 94,
    96

U

UNLOCK 35
UPDATE 35, 100
username 36
users 106

V

views 106

W

--without-pear 2

www.ingramcontent.com/pod-product-compliance
Lightning Source LLC
Chambersburg PA
CBHW051241050326
40689CB00007B/1021